FINDING BIGFOOT™

Meet the *Finding Bigfoot* team:
Cliff Barackman, James "Bobo" Fay,
Ranae Holland, and Matt Moneymaker!

ANIMAL PLANET

FINDING BIGFOOT™

EVERYTHING YOU NEED TO KNOW

BY MARTHA BROCKENBROUGH

FEIWEL AND FRIENDS

NEW YORK

A Feiwel and Friends Book
An Imprint of Macmillan

Printed in the United States of America by R. R. Donnelley & Sons Company,
Willard, Ohio. For information, address Feiwel and Friends,
175 Fifth Avenue, New York, N.Y. 10010.

Library of Congress Cataloging-in-Publication Data Available

ISBN: 978-1-250-04089-3 (hardcover)
2 4 6 8 10 9 7 5 3

ISBN: 978-1-250-04090-9 (paperback)
2 4 6 8 10 9 7 5 3 1

Book design by April Ward

Feiwel and Friends logo designed by Filomena Tuosto

First Edition: 2013

mackids.com

CONTENTS

I AM IN LOVE WITH MONSTERS. Always have been.

My first memories of bigfoot go back to when I was four or five years old. My dad, who is the best father you could ever ask for, joined something called the Indian Guides with me. We had to choose "little" and "big" Indian Guide names, and I almost went for Bigfoot. But even then, I was picky about words and didn't like how "Little Bigfoot" and "Big Bigfoot" sounded.

I've always been interested in these animals, though. They fascinate a lot of people because of what they represent: an archetype that gives us clues about our own origins. They also represent the monster in the human condition. And as much as we like the comforts of home, a lot of us want to be able to survive in the wild as a bigfoot does—that's why all those survivor shows are so successful.

While I didn't start searching for a real sasquatch until I was older, I'd always had a strong connection to the outdoors. Growing up in California, I'd go camping a lot with my family, especially in Sequoia National Park. We'd go looking for animal footprints. I never thought I'd see a bigfoot track, though. Back then, I thought the animal was a Pacific Northwest thing.

As I got older and started coming into my own self, I became even more drawn to weird things, as normal people bore me to tears. I like freaks and weirdos. I might look totally normal, and I have the dubious honor of being Bobo Fay's most normal friend (and his parents love me because it means there's hope for their boy). But I'm a pretty weird guy under it all. I was kicked out of the Boy Scouts because I didn't fall into line like I was supposed to.

In college, I rediscovered my fascination with bigfoot when I came across a collection of papers by cultural and physical anthropologists. They talked about stone heads depicting apes found on the Columbia River. These things were 1,000 years old, long before white men first visited the continent. What's more, there are no apes in North America. So what might these have represented? Furthermore, every Native American tribe has something like sasquatches as part of their mythology, even if they don't call them that. These animals are thrown in there with other real creatures: bears, foxes, and wolves. That's too big of a coincidence.

I was also impressed with the way physical anthropologists analyzed the Sierra Sounds, concluding that human beings aren't capable of producing noises like those. And there was Grover Krantz's convincing reconstruction of a sasquatch foot based on the tracks of a crippled specimen found in Bossburg, Washington.

I got hooked on the subject after that. I devoured every book in the library on it, and I started realizing that holy smokes, these things might be real! It wasn't so much a single piece of evidence that persuaded me, but rather, it was the consistency and internal congruency of all the data that had been gathered. People have been describing animals that look like bigfoot and act like bigfoot for centuries or more.

Bigfoot is real. But don't just take my word for it. Read this book. Consider the evidence. Look at the tracks. It's true that bigfoot doesn't yet have academic acceptance, but that's mostly a matter of ignorance, by which I mean ignoring data and evidence.

Even better, go look for bigfoot yourself. My favorite way to seek it is to sit in the woods and just listen. I calm my mind and bring a sense of awareness. I'm grounded when I'm out there in the woods. To search for bigfoot is to find . . . yourself.

I'm a professional teacher, and teachers are learners. My life is bigfoot now, and the only answer I have for why is that I love it. I didn't choose it. It chose me. I am in this for life.

—Cliff Barackman

PEOPLE SAY BIGFOOT DOESN'T EXIST.

That sasquatch is a legend. That we can forget about finding a yeti. It's a common misperception that all of these animals have been proven to be hoaxes, that "Bigfoot" was just some guy playing tricks on a Northern California road crew. But those doubters don't know what the stars of *Finding Bigfoot* know....

They don't know about the tracks . . .

About the noises and shining eyes in the woods at night . . .

About the deer carcasses with strangely snapped-off bones . . .

That long before the name "bigfoot" was applied to describe a creature that left giant tracks in the earth, human beings from around the world have been telling stories about an enormous, bipedal ape—a hairy, wild, and stunningly elusive mystery.

But thanks to Animal Planet's hit documentary show, which is entering its fourth fascinating season, people are starting to find out there is real science behind the possibility of the animal best known as bigfoot.

One key to the show's success is its four intrepid stars: Bigfoot Field Research Organization president Matt Moneymaker, researchers James "Bobo" Fay and Cliff Barackman, and skeptical scientist Ranae Holland.

These tireless searchers have covered vast territory, ranging from the shaggy woods of the Pacific Northwest to the nearly impenetrable jungles of Indonesia, taking viewers places they can only dream of visiting. The foursome brings an incredible depth of knowledge to their pursuit. They know what these animals like to eat, where they're most likely to be spotted, how they're likely to behave, and what sets them apart from other animals. They also know how to sniff out phonies and false leads.

What's more, the team is thorough in its search. They study photos and videos. They re-create sightings in the field, no matter how remote the territory. They use incredibly sophisticated technology, from night-vision cameras to drones, as well as clever techniques such as glow-in-the-dark powder. And they're not afraid to put their own bodies on the line, whether they're blasting sasquatch calls or waiting in the dark alone, hoping for a close encounter with the most elusive primate the world has ever known.

Without a doubt, if and when this team proves the existence of a giant North American ape, they will rewrite scientific history and satisfy a curiosity that has gripped humankind since we were telling stories around fire pits and painting our legends in caves.

You can follow the team both on the show and in this book, which shares the show's most mind-boggling encounters, historical and scientific background, new developments in sasquatch science, a collection of some of the strongest bigfoot evidence yet gathered, and practical advice you can put to use in your own adventures in finding bigfoot. It's enough to make even the most hardened skeptic take another look, and for people already fascinated by the creature, it's all the information you've ever wanted and so much more.

Chapter One
DOES BIGFOOT EXIST?

THE CASE FOR CRYPTIDS

Some people believe we know everything there is to know about this world. People who believe every inch of land has been conquered, every drop of ocean explored. And while it's true that adventurers have made their way around the globe, mapping the edges of oceans and continents, the heights of the mountains, the depths of the rivers and lakes, it's also true that scientists learn new things every day. What's more, we find new animals all the time.

Since 2012, for example, we have discovered all sorts of previously unknown creatures, including monkeys, frogs, sharks, and lizards—even primates. Would you believe there is such a thing as a poisonous spider with hooklike claws on each of its legs? A group of people exploring a cave in bigfoot Country—southern Oregon—stumbled across this family of spiders deep in the throat of a cave in 2012. The *Trogloraptor marchingtoni* was the first family of native North American spiders to be found in more than a century.

That same year, a Louisiana State University snake expert named Christopher Austin followed strange chirping noises while he was inside a

Papua New Guinea forest. It turns out a frog the size of the housefly, the world's tiniest vertebrate, was responsible for the singing. (The same professor has found several other species that hadn't yet been recognized by science, including other frogs, lizards, and parasites.)

There was a new primate recognized around the same time: the lesula monkey, a wise-looking creature with a grayish brown beard. This one was found in 2007 living as a school administrator's pet in the Democratic Republic of the Congo. Researchers studied its DNA to conclude it was an unrecognized species. It's already endangered because it's being hunted for its meat. It's only the second new kind of African monkey to be recognized in twenty-eight years, and it might have died out before scientists learned of its existence.

While most of these newly discovered creatures are small or live in remote places, history is full of animals once called legend that turned out to be real. The list of animals known by reputation first and recognized by science later includes gorillas, giant pandas, Komodo dragons, bonobos, megamouth sharks, giant geckos, and the okapi, a short-necked giraffe relative.

Here are a few especially important finds:

THE GIANT PANDA

This fuzzy creature was unknown outside of China until 1869, when a French missionary named Père Jean-Pierre Armand David described one that had been killed on a hunt. Westerners have been enthralled with pandas ever since. Today, they're exceedingly rare; only about 1,590 exist in the wild. But they could be an incredibly important species. Early in 2013, a component in giant panda blood was found to kill deadly bacteria six times faster than other antibiotics.

This is crucial because certain types of infections have become resistant to drugs we already have. If you think of your immune system as an army, and the drugs as bullets, drug resistance turns those once-effective bullets into soap bubbles. The panda blood could be an important key in fighting those tough and terrible infections.

And don't worry—scientists figured out how to re-create the panda substance in a lab. They decoded a panda's DNA and synthesized the substance, which is called cathelicidin-AM and probably helps keep the pandas healthy in the wild. Pandas aren't the only animals that have these disease-fighting powers. The same group of scientists found similar compounds in the slime of snails and certain amphibians.

THE GIANT SQUID

The giant squid is a literary legend. Vikings told tales of the terrible kraken, a sea monster big enough to wrap its tentacles around a ship and pull it below the waves. The *Odyssey*, an ancient poem, has a scary bit about a monster named Scylla that may well have been a giant squid.

But these creatures aren't just legends. In 2004, researchers in Japan shot the first-ever images of a live giant squid—nearly three thousand years after Homer wrote the *Odyssey*. That's a really long time for people to know about an animal without actually seeing a live specimen. The squids aren't the size of islands, but researchers found one squid that was fifty-nine feet long with eyes the size of dinner plates. There's a chance even bigger specimens are gliding beneath the waves.

Another animal, the saola (pronounced SOW-la), sometimes called the Asian unicorn because of its parallel sharp-tipped horns, was found in 1992 in north central Vietnam. Since then, scientists have observed this animal only four times; and none live in captivity. The saola is so rare that it is considered critically endangered, according to the World Wildlife Fund.

AN EXTINCT FISH—FOUND!

And then there's the coelacanth [SEE-luh-canth]. According to the fossil record, many species of this ancient fish lived between 360 million years ago and 80 million years ago. Then they went extinct, around the time that dinosaurs did.

This is why it was so very surprising when, in 1938, a self-trained naturalist named Marjorie Courtenay-Latimer found a coelacanth on a fishing dock. She brought it to a professor, who identified it by its distinctive shape and lobed fins. With that, a once-extinct fish was miraculously and officially back among the living, having somehow survived in secret in the Comoros Islands in the western Indian Ocean.

Equally surprising, in 1997, yet another variety was found in northern Sulawesi in Indonesia—nearly six thousand miles away from the islands in the western Indian Ocean where Courtenay-Latimer's fish was found. These two species of coelacanth are believed to be the only survivors of a once-varied type of fish, for now at least.

They're unique in many ways. For example, their skulls have a hinge that lets them open their

mouths superwide. They also have a "rostral organ" in their noses that is part of an electrosensory system. This works like an extra sense, allowing them to feel electromagnetic energy (sharks can do this, too). And they have fleshy, lobed fins that have bones inside of them, sort of like limbs.

Bigfooters love to offer up these examples as proof that bigfoot is a scientific possibility. Like the giant squid of legend, hairy two-legged creatures have appeared in folklore and stories around the world for ages. Like the coelacanth, there's a fossil record for similar creatures (hirsute human-like species that walk on two feet). And, as with the panda, there are real benefits to finding these mysterious creatures, wherever they might be hiding.

There's a controversial field of science that specializes in the study of "hidden" animals. It's called "cryptozoology," a word invented in the late 1950s by Bernard Heuvelmans, a zoologist. The word itself sounds pretty out there, but its meaning is straightforward: *crypto* means "hidden" and *zoology* means the "study of animals." It's related to paleontology, the study of prehistoric life, and both use reconstructions and evidence to build pictures of animals that haven't been seen or are no more. In addition to bigfoot, another famous cryptid, or hidden animal, is the Loch Ness Monster.

SPOTTED!
"It Was Kind of Creepy"

Howie Dagg lives in Hydaburg on Prince of Wales Island in Alaska. He and a neighbor had taken his truck out into the woods for a hike, hoping to relax and unwind after school. At first, they didn't even notice the tracks.

But then he got a closer look.

"I stopped and one of the tracks had toes, big toes in it," he said. "I stopped and we took some pictures . . . it was kind of creepy."

What's more, he and his friend felt as if they were being watched. Still, he felt skeptical, so he pushed on. Were they really bigfoot prints? He followed the trail all the way up the mountain.

At the top, where the road was choked with trees, he noticed a lot of branches had been snapped off about seven feet off the ground—a classic bigfoot sign.

The sun dipped behind the hill and it started to get dark, and that's when Howie's neighbor got scared, calling the creature a Gogit, which is a term used to describe a hairy giant in parts of Prince of Wales. Howie also had the willies, so they left.

The photos they took that day show prints 17.3 inches long and about 6.5 inches wide, the sort that might belong to a large male Sasquatch.

IS BIGFOOT REAL?

The truth is, no one knows for sure, although many people have strong opinions on the matter. We can only be absolutely certain there is such a creature as bigfoot when we have found one.

Otherwise, bigfoot remains a theoretical possibility. A theory is an explanation of something based on observations, experiments, and reasoning. When formed with care, theories are scientifically valid—even if they are not proven, and even when they apply to things we haven't seen.

Take black holes, for example. These are spots in space, big and small, where matter has been compressed (this can happen when a star dies). The compression of matter makes for an incredibly strong gravitational pull—a pull so strong nothing can escape it, not even light.

No one has ever seen a black hole (they're invisible!). No one has ever been inside one. But we can form theories about their existence because of careful, repeatable observations that have been made. As we learn more about physics, we might someday adjust our understanding and definition of black holes. But no one calls scientists crazy for believing such a thing exists because there is enough evidence to make it a reasonable thing to believe in.

Scientists ask questions, make observations, come up with smart guesses, devise experiments to test them, and consider the results thoughtfully. And that's exactly what you can do when it comes to bigfoot. There's nothing wrong with a healthy dose of skepticism. That's how scientists get smarter. And open minds are the only ones that can learn new things.

THE ARGUMENTS FOR BIGFOOT

Plenty of smart people believe bigfoot is alive and well and hiding from humanity. What makes them so sure there's a bigfoot when others say there's no such creature? It comes down to four things:

Folklore. One of the oldest surviving works of literature, *The Epic of Gilgamesh*, describes a hairy wild man named Enkidu. Similar tales of a hairy wild man who lives in the forest are part of many cultures around the world. Ancient cave paintings in California depict a Hairy Man and his family, and stories that go along with them sound very much like bigfoot tales. If no such animal exists, why would these stories be so common?

EVIDENCE PHOTO

Eyewitness accounts.

Thousands of people in the United States have reported seeing bigfoot. People in Canada have sasquatch sightings. In Nepal, people claim to have seen yetis. In Indonesia, a smaller version of a hairy man-like creature that walks on two feet is known as the Orang Pendek. There's also the Australian yowie. Many people who've had encounters are respected community members, including police officers and judges, who have a lot to lose by lying. If they're not lying, what did they see?

Physical evidence.

Although no one has found the body of a bigfoot, people have seen what they consider to be physical evidence. Footprints are among the best-known forms of evidence. The Bigfoot Field Research Organization (BFRO), for example, has collected more than seven hundred suspected Bigfoot prints. Many that come from different areas are strikingly similar in size and overall proportions.

Other physical evidence includes hair samples, some of which has not been identified as belonging to other known animals. Does it belong to bigfoot? We can only know for sure when there is a known specimen of Bigfoot to test against. bigfooters have also gathered what they believe are blood and stool samples.

And finally there are twisted-off branches, animal carcasses with cleanly broken bones, and clumps of sticks arranged into sleeping nests, all of which are considered evidence of the creature's presence in the woods.

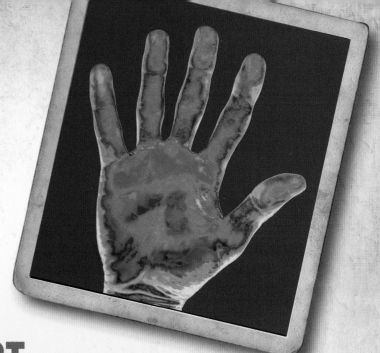

Photos, video, and audio recordings.
There are photographs, the famous Patterson-Gimlin film, thermal video recordings, and audio recordings said to be multiple bigfoots communicating with one another.

When you combine all of this evidence, believers say, you have a compelling picture of a large, hairy, bipedal animal that lives in remote forests and swamps.

BUILDING A BIGFOOT FROM A TRACK: ZADIG'S METHOD

In many ways, bigfoot hunters have to think like detectives, taking bits of information they have to make a picture of the animal as a whole. When you go through a process like this with the natural world, you use something called Zadig's Method, taking signs that are visible and deducing as much information as possible.

Baron Georges Cuvier, who created the modern field of paleontology, observed that if you saw a cloven hoof print, you could project a lot of information about the animal. For example, it would be a ruminant, meaning it is a mammal that chews plant material, softens it in the first part of its stomach, and then regurgitates it for a bit more chewing. But that's not all.

"This single track therefore tells the observer about the kind of teeth, the kind of jaws, the haunches, the shoulder, and the pelvis of the animal which has passed," he wrote in 1834.

This is what bigfoot believers are trying to do, and many people believe the evidence of bigfoot that has been gathered to date justifies the continued search.

THE ARGUMENTS AGAINST BIGFOOT

Bigfoot has an army of doubters. Their best argument is that people have been looking unsuccessfully for bigfoot for decades and, lately, even using sophisticated equipment such as cameras that can detect heat. If there really were such a creature, all those dedicated searchers using that great technology would have found proof.

That's a hard argument to counter, although die-hard squatchers will tell you the evidence they have gathered is proof. But if we define proof of bigfoot as an actual bigfoot, dead or alive (preferably alive, for the sake of the bigfoot), then we are about eight hairy feet and six hundred fifty pounds shy of certainty. Likewise, a DNA sequence confirmed by independent laboratories would also work as proof. Unless scientific standards relax, which isn't likely, you'd certainly need a holotype—a physical example of a Bigfoot, a Bigfoot body part, or DNA—for an official species to be named.

There are other arguments, as well.

What does a bigfoot eat?

Some people say there isn't enough food in places like the forests of the Pacific Northwest to support a bigfoot. That would be true if bigfoot eats a diet similar to gorillas, which are believed to survive on large quantities of plants and fruits, with the occasional insect thrown in. But even with known animals such as gorillas, we don't necessarily know everything there is to know about their diets.

For example, a study in 2010 raised the possibility that western lowland gorillas secretly eat meat. The study found DNA in their poop that came from monkeys and duikers (a small forest-dwelling antelope). The gorillas might have hunted or scavenged this meat, the study said. That would be a new and surprising find. We do have to stay somewhat skeptical, though—a good practice for scientists studying evidence. Other things could explain the DNA in the gorilla droppings. First, the ants that the gorillas ate might have fed on carcasses of these animals. The ants had the DNA in their bodies, and when the gorillas ate the ants, they got a secondhand dose. Second, the monkeys and duikers could have licked or otherwise come in contact with the feces. (Yuck!)

The point, though, is that it's possible bigfoot's diet extends beyond the salad bar. Two other great apes, chimpanzees and bonobos, do eat meat. Likewise, bigfooters argue the creatures are omnivores, living on plants as well as deer and other animals consumed by predators at the top of the food chain, such as cougars, wolves, and bears.

Questions about habitat

A trickier argument is that everywhere else in the world, large apes live in tropical habitats. The Pacific Northwest and Canada, two bigfoot and sasquatch hotspots, are anything but hot when it comes to the weather. It doesn't mean bigfoot is impossible in such climates. But it does make them different from the world's other apes. There are primates that buck this tropical trend, though. The Japanese macaque, *Macaca fuscata*, is found in the same latitude as northern California. Those monkeys even survive snowy winters (which is why they're known informally as snow monkeys).

The agony of the feet

Many skeptics believe there are other explanations for the evidence the bigfoot believers have gathered. A huge footprint, for example, might actually be multiple footprints. If you stepped in wet sand and then moved your foot down and made a new print, you might be able to create what looks like a very long foot. When this happens, it's called a "double-stepped" footprint. Likewise, a bear footprint in the snow that's melted or sublimated (evaporated without melting first) might look larger than the original print.

A plague of hoaxes

Finally, bigfoot hoaxes have done a lot of damage to the cause. There are many accounts of people faking tracks well enough to convince experts, only to reveal the shenanigans afterward. Other hoaxers have frozen ape suits and dressed up in costume for a misleading run through the woods.

A cast of possible bigfoot footprint

The many high-profile hoaxes over the years have swirled like drops of black ink in a cup of milk, discoloring the whole pursuit for many sensible people.

SPOTTED!
A Flying Piece of Wood from "Out of Nowhere"

Nyna Fleury drives a cab in Alaska's Prince of Wales Island, making regular trips back and forth during the night. On one of those wee-hours trips, she had a passenger with her.

"Out of nowhere, this piece of wood comes flying at us," she said. "It hit the front end of the car and cracked my windshield all the way across."

Something big had to have thrown it because the impact shook her entire van. Nyna wanted to stop, but her frightened passenger urged her on.

She returned to investigate the next day and found the piece of wood. It smelled putrid. She looked up into a nearby tree and saw a pair of big green eyes looking at her from inside a "humongous" body.

There's no way it was a bear, she said.

"It's a strange story," Bobo Fay said, "but sasquatches are strange animals. They do weird things."

BRINGING SCIENCE TO THE SEARCH

For bigfoot to become an official species, we need concrete evidence that can be examined systematically and thoroughly. We also need a theory that explains why, despite a lot of searching, no one has ever found bigfoot, a skeleton, or even a few remaining bones that once belonged to the creature.

Cliff Barackman has advice for bigfooters about how to take a scientific approach to the search: Follow the scientific method. Here's how that model of thinking works:

1. Ask a question.

2. Research. Look for evidence and other clues that could point to an answer.

3. Take a guess at an answer. This guess is called a hypothesis.

4. Create an experiment to see if your hypothesis could be right.

5. Execute the experiment. Were you right? Repeat the experiment to verify. If you're not, start again at step 2.

6. Write your experiment and results, and share them with other researchers to see if they find the same thing.

The goal of these observations—or any scientific observations, really—is to establish a set of reliable facts. Using those, we can then conduct further research. It's sort of like building with LEGOs. You start with a foundation and keep adding to that, removing blocks or theories that have been disproved with additional observations and experiments.

Many people in traditional science are so skeptical of bigfoot they don't even bother to consider new evidence. But this doesn't mean science itself is a jerk. Science can be a bigfooter's best friend. Many kinds of science can potentially come into play: paleontology, the study of prehistoric life; anthropology, the study of human behavior and cultures; kinesiology, the study of human movement; primatology, the study of primates; and of course genetics and wildlife biology.

Generally speaking, the more you know about science, the more opportunities and insight you will have in life. When it comes to bigfoot specifically, the more you know about what sort of animal bigfoot might be, the more you know about how and where a bigfoot might live. That insight gives you a better chance at encountering a bigfoot at last.

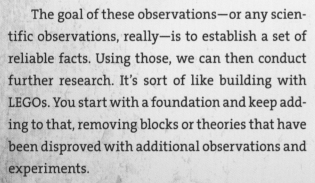
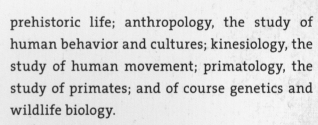

IS BIGFOOT SCIENTIFICALLY POSSIBLE? MAYBE!

To establish that bigfoot is a possibility, scientists might first pose a "continuity test." If an animal like bigfoot has been alive at any point, it has to be a link somewhere in the evolutionary chain. Complex animals don't just magically appear. They are the offspring and relatives of animals that have come before them.

Going from the descriptions of bigfoot given by people who've had encounters and by Native American "hairy man" tales, we can take an educated guess that bigfoot is an ape-like primate. Primates are in a category of animals, called an order, that includes monkeys, apes, and humans, as well as other mammals.

Although North America's fossil record includes primates, and although giant mammals flourished on the continent, there isn't at this point any fossil evidence for giant apes in North America. We have paleontological evidence of plenty of amazing, huge mammals, including giant sloths, woolly mammoths, and saber-toothed cats. But no apes, at least not in the fossil record. Asia has fossil apes. South America has fossil monkeys. So it's a troubling blank spot.

But this isn't as devastating for bigfoot's case as it might sound. We know there are apes in Africa, which means there had to be earlier forms, too. Even so, it still took scientists ages to dig up fossil ancestors for African apes.

What's more, the Northwest, which is home to many a bigfoot sighting, is famously wet and not as fossil rich as drier areas. It's possible—if giant apes did live there—that no remains were fossilized. And that's okay. Even without fossils, we can still take what we know about primates and make intelligent guesses about Bigfoot's diet, life span, and behavior.

And, because we are arming ourselves with science, we can eliminate some of the goofier Bigfoot lore, which claims they are space alien scouts or able to disappear into a different dimension magically at will. People are of course free to believe what they want, but it's best for any serious bigfooter to focus on theories that are grounded in verifiable observations.

Using science, we can also pinpoint where bigfoot might be most likely to live: a habitat that has enough food and other resources. We can examine evidence, including footprints, hair, and other biological samples, as well as sounds, pictures, and videos.

And we can share our research with other seekers, such as the Bigfoot Field

Researchers Organization. Even though much of the scientific world has rejected the possibility of Bigfoot, real scientists are—to this day—opening their laboratories to evidence gathered in the field. Late in 2012, for example, the Oxford-Lausanne Collateral Hominid Project at the University of Oxford in the United Kingdom invited people to do just this. A professor of human genetics there requested samples—especially hair—suspected to belong to Bigfoot for DNA analysis. It's exciting to see a partnership between universities and Bigfoot investigators in the field. If anything will get us closer to finding bigfoot, it's teamwork such as this.

FAMOUS FANS OF BIGFOOT

Bigfoot has many famous fans.

Theodore "Teddy" Roosevelt became the twenty-sixth president of the United States—and also the youngest—when he took office after the assassination of President William McKinley. He led an exciting and sometimes sad life. His first wife, Alice, and his mom died on the same day in 1884. Understandably heartbroken, he spent the next two years mostly riding horseback on his ranch, which was in the Badlands of the Dakota Territory.

His book, *The Wilderness Hunter*, was published in 1893, and included a story about a hunter in Idaho who'd been attacked by a hairy monster. Bigfooters sometimes point to this incident as a sighting.

Another famous fan was Mark Twain, who wrote books such as *The Adventures of Tom Sawyer*, *The Adventures of Huckleberry Finn*, and *The Prince and the Pauper*, and who also argued for simplified spelling rules that would have saved you a lot of studying if people had actually listened to his ideas.

Twain once wrote a pretend interview with bigfoot, whom he called "the mysterious 'wild man' out there in the West." He said he felt sorry for bigfoot, whose life had been one of suffering, disappointment, and exile. This doesn't necessarily mean he thought there was such a thing as sasquatch, but rather, that he liked the idea of the creature and thought it represented something true about human beings and the shabby way we sometimes treat one another.

Daniel Boone, the American frontier explorer, actually claimed to have shot a bigfoot when he was in the Kentucky forest that now bears his name. He described his quarry as a ten-foot-tall ape, which he called a yahoo. It's hard to tell if this is a true story or a tall (and hairy) tale.

The actor Jimmy Stewart, most famous for playing George Bailey in *It's a Wonderful Life*, might not have been a believer in bigfoot, but he helped play a role in an abominable snowman mystery in 1959. A yeti hunter named Peter Byrne had visited the Pangboche monastery in Nepal to

James Stewart

Matt LeBlanc is a bigfoot believer!

study what was supposedly a yeti hand. Byrne's own fingers were a bit sticky, and he replaced a phalanx and thumb bone from the yeti hand with human bones. Then he met with Stewart and his wife, Gloria, in Calcutta and passed the stolen bones on to the Hollywood star, who smuggled them to London. Ultimately, experts deemed the bones to be human. Weirdly shaped. But human, after all.

Bigfoot's most famous modern friend, though, might be the actor Matt LeBlanc, who played Joey on the TV show *Friends*. He's told interviewers he's a fan of bigfoot and the search for the creature, and Ellen DeGeneres even gave him his own bigfoot statue. (Don't worry—it wasn't life-size. He'd never fit that in a suitcase!)

SPOTTED!
Screams from All Sides

Osh Lang-Edenshaw rode his four-wheeler as far into the woods near Hydaburg, Alaska, as he could before parking it and heading into the backcountry on foot. It was early in the morning and the twelve-year-old boy had planned to do a little solo hunting. He was tracking a deer, maybe a bit farther into the wilderness than he should have.

"It kept going," he said, "and I got to the point where I thought I should turn around. And as soon as I turned around, I heard those loud screams coming in three directions, and I just froze."

Thirty feet away from him stood a creature the *Finding Bigfoot* team estimated to be as big as nine feet tall in a reenactment.

"I looked right in its eyes," he said. "The most terrifying sight I've ever seen in my life." Shaken, he looked down and closed his eyes. When he opened them again a few seconds later, he heard heavy thumps. The screams from other creatures continued.

"It was just a flashback of my life," he said. "I honestly thought I was gonna die. It was bad."

Chapter Two
A LOOK AT THE EVIDENCE

THE BEST EVIDENCE FOR BIGFOOT

Over the years, people have cataloged all sorts of evidence for bigfoot, including prints made by feet, hands—and even a couple of bottoms. Evidence includes audio recordings of sasquatch shrieks and video recordings of squatches on the move.

Although no evidence is as compelling as an actual bigfoot, the best that's been gathered over the years is fascinating and guarantees you'll always have something meaty to talk about with your friends at lunch. As mystery meat goes, bigfoot is much more palatable than what they serve in the cafeteria.

Note: There is no evidence whatsoever anywhere to suggest school cafeterias serve bigfoot meat in their food.

THE HAIRY MAN PICTOGRAPHS

Plenty of people believe bigfoot is a made-up creature, a hoax from the 1950s meant to pull the legs of gullible loggers.

Even if every sighting of a bigfoot since then is a hoax, it's hard to explain Painted Rock. This is a five-hundred- to one-thousand-year-old archaeological site in California's Sierra Nevada range. The Yokut tribal members who lived there were called the People of Painted Rock (O-ching'-i-ta), which shows how significant the site was to their culture.

Anthropologists believe this cave art was meant to explain the origin of human beings and our various traits. The pictures show a hairy man family with two parents and a child. He looks a lot like bigfoot, with shaggy hair, a big, human-like body, and a ridge on top of his head known as a sagittal crest. The traditional Yokut stories describe the creature as a nocturnal hunter that knocks on wood, whistles, and eats both animals and plants—the same as many modern accounts.

White people first described the site in 1889, and a tribal elder living there identified the creatures depicted as hairy man long before any of the famous California bigfoot sightings occurred. While it is true that no fossils of North American

apes have been found, it's hard to dismiss the significance of ancient pictures of apes in Native American sites, especially when these pictures are meant to explain how human beings came to walk on two feet. Tribal lore is full of real animals these people witnessed: crows, eagles, lizards, owls, coyotes, condors. So if they did not see a hairy man, what inspired this creature?

What's more, First Nations art includes ceremonial masks and carved stones that resemble apes. What would their model be if there were no North American apes?

As fascinating as these paintings are, so are the parallels between First Nations lore and real behavior of apes in the wild. Kathy Moskowitz Strain, an archaeologist for the U.S. Forest Service, has written about the pictographs and the accompanying tales in a book called *Giants, Cannibals & Monsters: Bigfoot in Native Culture*. As typical narratives go, parents warn their kids not to swim in the river at night, lest they run into bigfoot. They also warn that a hungry bigfoot who can't find other animals to eat might choose to dine on children— something chimpanzees have been known to do in the wild when they can't find enough food in the forest.

SPOTTED!
"Honored" by bigfoot

Brenda Leask, her cousin, and her aunt were out deer hunting, and her cousin had just blown a deer call when a tall, hairy creature stepped out from behind a tree.

"It was so big," she said, estimating its height at over eight feet. "I couldn't believe what I just saw." Momentarily stunned into silence, she and her cousin finally acknowledged what had just happened.

"We were there about five minutes," she said, "and we told my aunt, 'We've got to go.'"

But it wasn't a traumatic experience. Leask is a member of the Tlingit tribe and her clan's history is tied to the sasquatch itself. "You feel honored to have had this creature show itself to you. It was such a profound moment in my life."

BOSSBURG TRACKS

A little town in Stevens County, Washington, has played a big part in the hunt for bigfoot evidence. Its name is Bossburg, and it lies on the east bank of the mighty Columbia River, not too far south of the Canadian border. It's a ghost town now, and it was never big—just eight hundred people at its peak.

But it was an interesting place to be late in 1969, when the first of some very curious bigfoot tracks appeared. A couple of things made them stand out. First, they were near a garbage dump— an unusual thing for a normally reclusive bigfoot. Second, these footprints revealed something sad and stunning: Although the left foot was normal for a Squatch, measuring seventeen inches long and seven inches wide, the creature that made them had a deformed right foot.

The bum foot gave the creature its nickname: Cripplefoot, as well as an explanation for what it might be doing so close to people. Because it was injured or deformed, it couldn't make its way in the wilderness. It also gave scientists a reason to take a close look at the prints, which were extremely detailed. One toe was so bent, for example, that it hardly left an impression in the soil. A pair of bumps on the outside edge of the foot revealed the bones there might have been broken.

John Napier, a famous primate expert from the Smithsonian Institution, believed the deformity almost guaranteed the tracks were authentic. "It's very difficult to conceive of a hoaxer so subtle, so knowledgeable—and so sick—who would deliberately fake a footprint of this nature," he said. "I suppose it is possible, but it is so unlikely that I am prepared to discount it."

They also intrigued Grover Krantz, a professor of physical anthropology at Washington State University and the first academic to seriously investigate the possibility of bigfoot. Based on the deformity, Krantz figured out the anatomy of a sasquatch foot, and from there, how heavy bigfoot might be based on its foot.

In an article in *Northwest Anthropological Research Notes* from the spring of 1972, Krantz pointed out differences in human and Sasquatch feet.

In general, the sasquatch foot differs from man's in having greatly enlarged ankle bones, especially the heel, very short metatarsals, and a more nearly equal set of toes. These characteristics are all logical requirements for an otherwise human foot adapted to a body weight of five hundred pounds or more. These characteristics are also evident in preserved footprints.

Bigfoot footprint cast

In all, lifelong sasquatch hunter René Dahinden found 1,089 of these footprints, and whatever creature made them had to step twice over a barbed wire fence forty-three inches high—something a human would have a hard time doing.

Even today, they're among the favorite pieces of evidence that persuade bigfoot seekers the creature is out there, even though the experts studying them back in the day didn't agree on every point. Napier, the Smithsonian expert, thought the tracks showed bigfoot had a human-like foot. Krantz did not.

What makes the tracks a tricky piece of evidence, though, are a couple of hoaxes that happened around the same time and place. It doesn't necessarily mean the tracks are phony. People could have capitalized on them to profit from hoaxes of their own. But they made the tracks smell a bit fishy as a result. (See Chapter 9.)

BIGFOOT WITNESS PHOTO

THE PATTERSON-GIMLIN FILM

For some, Friday, October 20, 1967, is the biggest day in bigfoot history. Roger Patterson and Bob Gimlin had left Patterson's home state of Washington, where the two were shooting a movie about bigfoot. They heard of some tracks in California and went to check them out—but the rain had beaten them there and washed the footprints away. It was disappointing, to be sure, but the two men decided to make the best of it. They set up camp and rode into the Bluff Creek area on horseback, taking footage of the beautiful fall scenery as they rode.

That afternoon, their horses freaked out.

Roger took a tumble. And that's when he saw it, sixty to eighty feet away. A bigfoot.

The *Los Angeles Times*'s *West Magazine* described what he saw:

Its head was very human, though considerably more slanted, and with a large forehead and wide, broad nostrils. Its arms hung almost to its knees when it walked. Its hair was two to four inches long, brown underneath, lighter at the top, and covering the entire body except for the face around the nose, mouth, and cheek. And it was female.

Patterson jumped up, turned on his camera, and ran toward the creature. Gimlin stood with his gun ready (although he apparently had no plans to shoot unless it was necessary). Patterson captured footage until his film ran out. Too spooked to reload, they took plaster casts of prints that were fourteen and a half inches, and so deep Gimlin had to jump off a fallen tree to make similar impressions with his cowboy boots. They sent the film to a town in Washington called Yakima to be developed, and when they met with other committed Bigfoot researchers (including John Green and René Dahinden—see Chapter 5), people agreed they had all the proof they needed. Patterson, who was sort of a schemer in his business dealings, even refrained from selling the movie to the highest bidder because he was warned it would lead to ridicule and rejection.

The footage, which lasts about one minute, is imperfect. The first few seconds show nothing but the ground rushing by, because Patterson is running. When he finally tilts the camera up toward "Patty," the name people have given the creature on the film, it's shaky at first. The footage does get more stable and shows a tall, hairy creature with a pointed head stride by, glance over her right shoulder, and turn toward the woods.

Supporters of the movie say the footage would be impossible to fake. Not only would such a costume have been too sophisticated to fake at the time—the chest and shoulders of the animal are too broad to be human, the arms are too long, and muscles are visible moving under the fur. They also say her gait isn't human and is too swift to be faked. Both men involved believed what they'd seen was real and not someone in a suit.

Bob Titmus, a taxidermist who studied and collected many suspected bigfoot tracks over the years, visited the site after the footage was shot and took casts of ten footprints. He noted each one was different. The toes moved. The way they gripped the soil varied. They showed different weight placement. In short, they hadn't been made by a rigid, carved template. They appeared to him as if they'd been laid down by a walking creature.

But, as it's turned out, the movie hasn't been universally acknowledged as slam-dunk scientific sasquatch proof.

For starters, the footage is low quality and brief, because Patterson used most of his film taking nature shots. What's more, he didn't know the film speed (which determines the sensitivity to light) he used for taking the movie, which is a piece of information you need to have to know whether a human in a costume could have taken those steps. There's been quite a bit of debate about the f-stop the camera had been set at. Scientists such as Idaho State University's Jeffrey Meldrum and the late Grover Krantz have made strong cases that it was shot at a speed that would make it impossible for humans to fake the footage, but others remain unconvinced.

Since then, it's been studied many times over the years, with mixed results. John Napier, the anatomist and anthropologist who was the director of primate biology at the Smithsonian Institution, dissected the footage in a book called *Bigfoot.*

"There is little doubt that the scientific evidence taken collectively points to a hoax of some kind," he wrote.

He spotted several problems: a person could have walked that way, the center of gravity is more human than ape, and the length of the steps didn't match up with the footprints Patterson and Gimlin found.

Frank Beebe, a naturalist and the illustrator at the Royal British Columbia Museum, raised other questions. Even though the animal has breasts, she walks like a man. She also has a distinct sagittal crest—that's the pointy part on the top of her head. Animals that eat leaves, like gorillas, have heads like these because the strong muscles required for chewing low-calorie, fiber-filled leaves connect to the skull. To digest all this fiber, these animals also have long intestines and a big belly to house these guts. Patty doesn't.

On the whole, Beebe found the movie "rather good, very interesting," even if it wasn't ultimately persuasive, he wrote in his notes. "It just could be genuine and the darn thing for real, although the chance, indeed, the likelihood of a hoax is very high."

Another critic, David Daegling, author of *Bigfoot Exposed*, also objected to the sagittal crest, saying only male primates have these. Other experts dispute this, saying these are more noticeable in males, but that some female primates have them.

Scientists at the American Museum of Natural History and the University of British Columbia ruled the movie a fake. So did Bernard Heuvelmans, a scientist and explorer known as the father of cryptozoology. His reason? Patty has curving buttocks and apes don't. The counterargument: Apes aren't bipedal and don't need a muscular bottom to keep their torsos upright, as a two-footed walker such as sasquatch does.

All these objections aside, the film hasn't been universally rejected by scientists. In 1994, Russian scientists from the Darwin Museum in Moscow endorsed the movie.

What's more, no one has definitively proved the film is a hoax. And certainly for bigfoot believers, the movie is just what it looks like: proof that sasquatch are out there, just waiting to be found.

SAGITTAL CREST

SPOTTED!
Sasquatch with a Sweet Tooth

Mike Greene is a bigfooter from North Carolina. He's worked with the Bigfoot Field Researchers Organization and other groups for about twenty years, but never hit pay dirt until he started coming to a particular campground.

The night he had his encounter, the campground was empty. He'd put up his tent and was sacked out until three o'clock in the morning, when a plopping noise woke him up.

"It sounded like somebody dropping a water balloon on the floor," he said.

Then the wheezing Darth Vader breaths started—right over his tent.

"And then something cuffed the top of the tent and I whacked the side of the tent back and it ran off."

He heard a rustling noise below and figured the creature was watching him. So he decided to grab his tripod and camera from the car, which was parked about eighty-five feet away. He mounted his thermal camera and drove off, waited two hours, and then returned.

The camera battery was dead, but he'd captured a blurry thermal image of a creature stealing a candy bar from a stump.

SIERRA SOUNDS

Alan Berry was a geologist, Vietnam veteran, and former newspaper reporter who wrote about his bigfoot encounters in the Sierra Mountains. He'd been visiting a remote deer hunters' camp and had become aware of "a 'presence' . . . of several creatures who were crafty enough to avoid observation, but freely vocalized and whistled, several times . . . and left big prints of bare feet around in the snow and pine mat."

He'd heard of similar strange experiences by other hunters. So he brought what was then a state-of-the-art Sony portable tape recorder and some plaster of Paris to capture evidence of this elusive creature.

On his first visit, nothing happened, although he did see some old footprints that he dismissed as a joke by other hunters.

The second time in, things were different.

"As dusk became dark night, something approached camp from a ridge above, rapping on wood or rocks as it came, and when it arrived, two voices that I could discern . . . vocalized, and the sounds carried through the trees as I have never heard human voices carry ever before or since.

"And it whistled," he wrote, "a clear, beautiful whistle like a bird might make, between its kind, and at one point back and forth and with us."

He recorded the exchange and cast several footprints. He looked around for evidence it was all a hoax, including in other hunters' belongings. But he came home stumped.

Experts have found the recordings to be intriguing.

The tapes hadn't been altered, prerecorded, or rerecorded, and the vocal range went beyond what an average human male could produce, according to a presentation by Dr. R. Lynn Kirlin, a professor of electrical engineering at the University of Wyoming. Kirlin made this presentation at an "Anthropology of the Unknown" symposium at the University of British Columbia.

Later, a retired U.S. Navy linguistics expert named R. Scott Nelson listened to the tapes. Nelson spent his career as a cryptolinguist—someone trained to recognize coded language. He's convinced the recordings have captured a real language.

On Bigfootsounds.com, he wrote:

We have verified that these creatures use language by the human definition of it. The months of hard work that we have put into the study of the Berry/Morehead tapes are finally coming to fruition. The analysis is finished, although I am still working on parts of the final write-up such as frequency count tables, morpheme lists, etc.

I believe that the study of these tapes will never (and should never) end. With the recognition and acceptance that these creatures do indeed speak and understand a complex language, a greater effort will be made to collect voice recordings and our analysis of the language will improve. Now that we have a precedent and techniques established for this study, this process will certainly become easier.

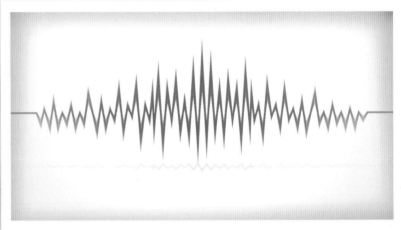
Here's an example of a frequency wave.

JACOBS PHOTOGRAPHS

Technology has improved since the days when people measured bigfoot tracks with pieces of cardboard. Cameras are more sophisticated than ever. It's possible to set them up in the woods so that they take pictures when something passes by. These are called "trail cameras," and on rare occasions, they capture fascinating evidence.

The Jacobs Photographs might be the most famous of suspected bigfoot pictures captured by trail camera. They were taken in 2007 by a hunter named Rick Jacobs, who'd set up the camera in the Allegheny National Forest in northwest Pennsylvania.

The pictures, lit by an invisible infrared flash, depict a smallish, hairy creature bent toward the ground, almost as though it's walking on all fours.

Some people have dismissed it as a "mangy

This trail camera is the eyes of the forest!

though, wildlife photography is a difficult business. The images we often see in documentaries and on television are very often staged in conditions that don't occur naturally, making us expect to see any animal we wish in high-definition video. But it's much harder than this, and plenty of animals we *know* to exist are rarely photographed in the wild. One example is the wolverine, a member of the weasel family that looks a bit like a four-foot, sixty-pound bear, and is known to rove some of the same habitat a sasquatch is thought to occupy.

For now at least, it is worth paying close attention to what's captured by trail cameras—one good shot could change everything about people's willingness to accept the possibility of Bigfoot.

bear," but bigfoot researchers disagree. The camera also took pictures of bear cubs, and these look quite different. People have analyzed the pictures and compared the arm and leg length of bears with that of primates, and concluded the creature was built more like a primate than a bear.

The images are important for a couple of reasons, Cliff Barackman says. "The first reason is they're close and fairly clear. There are very few if any good photographs of juvenile sasquatches. Another reason the Jacobs Photographs are important is because it actually shows that sasquatches can be captured by trail cameras. . . . It's encouraging to people like me."

Despite the improvement in technology,

A real wolverine doesn't quite resemble the X-Men character, does it?

SKOOKUM CAST

Not all famous sasquatch prints come from the creature's feet. Many people believe that in 2000, a male bigfoot left a body print in the muddy Skookum Meadow of the Gifford Pinchot National Forest in Washington State. This print—made into what is called the Skookum Cast—was found by Matt Moneymaker and other members of the

Bigfoot Field Researchers Organization.

It happened on September 22, 2000, a briskly cold clear day. Frost covered the ground, and members of the team were checking fruit traps they'd baited with melons, apples, and peanuts. A report on their Web site explains how they'd done all sorts of other things designed to attract a bigfoot, broadcasting squatch calls, playing tapes of children playing and babies crying.

At nine o'clock in the morning, three team members checked the traps. Three of six apples were missing at one of the sites, which was surrounded by old tracks of elk, deer, bears, and coyotes. That's when the team members noticed an unusual impression at the edge of a muddy pool.

"Then suddenly it dawns what animal caused it," the field notes said.

They alerted base camp and everyone came to check out the print. They agreed an animal sat down at the edge of the mud and leaned toward the fruit, using its left forearm for support. It grabbed the fruit with its right hand. People wondered right away why the bigfoot didn't just bend over for the fruit. One explanation readily sprang to mind—that the creature didn't want to leave tracks. It was also possible that the animal was being cautious and sitting to observe the situation, especially because the muddy site was near the camp.

"If these animals have been avoiding confrontations with humans for thousands of years, might this behavior—avoidance of leaving distinctive footprints—be an ancient survival strategy?" the report said.

This stealth behavior seems unique to sasquatch, the report said.

Several experienced sasquatch field researchers in the group noted that they had likely seen this behavior before—track patterns suggesting the animals did not want to leave obvious tracks behind. . . . This is in contrast to most other large mammals, which usually don't make special efforts, or take special paths, to avoid leaving tracks behind. We also noted that in cases where lots of clear sasquatch tracks have been found, the locations were usually in very remote areas that saw little to no human traffic—such as Bluff Creek in the late 1950s.

The researchers made a cast using more than two hundred pounds of plaster. The whole thing is huge: more than three-and-a-half feet by five feet long. That same expedition netted investigators' voice recordings and blurry seventeen-inch footprints.

Afterward, a team of scientists and bigfoot researchers examined the cast, including Jeffrey Meldrum, a professor at Idaho State University; Dr. Grover Krantz, a retired physical anthropologist from Washington State University; Dr. John Bindernagel, a Canadian wildlife biologist; John Green, a retired Canadian journalist and author; and Dr. Ron Brown, exotic animal handler and health care administrator.

Idaho State University issued a press release about the find, quoting Meldrum: "While not definitively proving the existence of a species of North American ape, the cast constitutes significant and compelling new evidence that will hopefully stimulate further serious research and investigation into the presence of these primates in the Northwest mountains and elsewhere."

The cast is unique because it's the only imprint believed to represent a partial bigfoot body. Searchers have found hands, knuckles—even bigfoot butt prints—but this was the first time they'd snagged a body, and the dimensions of it suggested it was forty to fifty percent bigger than a six-foot-tall human. A careful cleaning revealed hair impressions on the creature's bottom and thighs, as well as a longer fringe of hair

on the forearm. The heel had fingerprint-like skin ridges, Meldrum noted. It looked like other sasquatch footprints. He could also make out a heel, ankle, and Achilles tendon that looked like the hundreds of other alleged sasquatch footprints he'd studied.

The Achilles tendon and big rump are things you'd find on creatures that walk upright, something that led Daris Swindler, a University of Washington primate anatomist who studied the cast, to say, "In my opinion, the Skookum body cast is that of an upright descendant of Gigantopithecus [an extinct giant ape]" (see Chapter 3).

But that wasn't all. A biomedical research scientist named Dr. Wolf Henner Fahrenbach studied hair samples from the scene and on the cast. Most were deer, elk, coyote, and bear. But one hair—based on characteristics of other samples collected in Sasquatch sightings—was distinctly primate. Its owner? According to Fahrenbach, sasquatch.

Again, not everyone agrees with this interpretation, but the fact remains that well-trained experts are convinced.

SPOTTED!

The Long Arm of the Law Not Long Enough

Rural northern Georgia is lush, a mix of small farming communities surrounded by vast tracts of national forest. The Chattahoochee National Forest has a reputation for being a bigfoot hotspot. The region even has petroglyphs—rock paintings—by early Native Americans that show them interacting with a bigfoot-like creature.

So it was not a surprise to the *Finding Bigfoot* team that a Georgia State patrol car captured what appears to be Sasquatch footage on its dashboard camera.

Mary Scott was a passenger in the car on the night it happened. It was late and the road was empty.

"We were coming this way about fifty-five miles an hour," she said. "It's pitch black, so it seemed like we were doing a hundred.

"All of a sudden with no notice whatsoever, this very tall, very furry, very fast creature comes from that side of the road," she said.

The trooper braked, turned around, and put on his flashing lights. They both jumped out of the car. He drew his gun and identified himself, but to no avail.

"Whatever it was, was gone," she said.

NEW YORK BABY SASQUATCH

Just what was that creature swinging nimbly from a tree branch in the Catskill Mountains in 1997?

In a short video that's been dubbed "New York Baby Bigfoot" footage, sharp-eyed viewers can make out what appears to be a large figure move beneath a tree to give a smaller creature a boost into the high branches, where it swings around like some sort of ape.

The footage was captured by accident on private land that used to be an apple orchard and still has a few fruit-bearing trees growing. The cameraman, Doug Pridgen, was sitting around a campfire at a music festival shooting footage of his friends. Pets weren't allowed at the festival. People who'd brought dogs (and parrots and iguanas, apparently) were turned away, so it seems unlikely anyone could've smuggled in a gibbon, which is an ape about the size of the creature on the film.

The *Finding Bigfoot* team tried to re-create the footage, but Cliff Barackman wasn't nimble enough to ape the ape.

"I've spent a lot of time around gymnastics in general," he said. "My ex-wife was a gymnastics instructor. I've seen it again and again. The best gymnasts in the world, they cannot duplicate what I've seen in that video. So what we have here is either a case of a pet ape or a sasquatch, possibly an adult and a juvenile."

Gregg Dancho, director at Connecticut's Beardsley Zoo, agreed the footage is neither bear nor human.

It's clearly something that's brachiating through the trees, hanging like a monkey. People don't realize how big our wild areas are. People have a tendency of thinking, you know, the United States, we're all closed in and there's not many wild areas. When you actually go out in the woods you see how much, how big these areas are, so I wouldn't be surprised if something's out there that hasn't been discovered yet. I would not be surprised at all.

(That said, Dancho stated later in a Connecticut newspaper interview that he does not believe in bigfoot.)

THE LONDON TRACKWAY

In February 2012, a man named Max Roy was taking a walk in London, Oregon, when a passerby told him about some bigfoot tracks. Roy went to check them out and took photos, but felt a bit spooked, so he went home. He couldn't get them out of this mind, though, so he got in touch with a bigfooter named Toby Johnson, who inspected the tracks for himself and immediately contacted Cliff Barackman.

"I was definitely interested in the find, especially after seeing one of Max's photographs of the prints in the ground," Cliff said. "I instructed him what to document, and how to cast all four prints."

Cliff couldn't check them out by himself, though. The next day, he had to teach students about how he uses the scientific method. That's when he got another call from Johnson. It wasn't

Bigfoot footprint cast alongside a dollar bill gives perspective to the print size.

mold. Cliff's Web site has photos of each footprint cast, in addition to detailed notes about their depth, shape, and how closely they correlate to other suspected bigfoot tracks.

The tracks are a unique event in bigfoot history because so many were found and cast at one time. Cliff is still studying the prints to see what they might reveal. But they remain his most important piece of evidence.

It is, by far, the most significant thing I've been directly involved with. The casts and photographs from the event continue to astound me. I have spent countless hours poring over the minute details of the casts and pictures taken at the site, and I continually learn more from them at every inspection.

It's not just me, either. Every bigfooter that has seen the casts has walked away from inspecting them with the impression that these are probably the real deal.

just four tracks. It was more than a hundred. As soon as Cliff finished teaching, he set out for London and asked a friend to meet him with two hundred pounds of Hydrocal to take casts of the prints.

They eventually cast 72 of the 122 found. They also photographed the series, which appears to show feet in motion through the mud, as opposed to static prints made by a hoaxer with a rigid

SPOTTED!

"This Creature Has Opened My Door"

Carolyn Bridges and her husband, Bill, live in Florida, home to thick forests, treacherous swamps, and stories of a foul-smelling creature called the skunk ape.

One night, a horrible growl ripped Carolyn out of sleep. "I was spooked and I touched Bill and kind of [shook] him and he doesn't move," she said. "I'm kind of in shock here because this thing sounded monstrous."

And it sounded close. As close as her porch.

When she checked the next day, she was in for a shock.

"Here was a huge handprint," she said. The thumb and fingers were huge and long, she said. The attached arm was wide and greasy and left a hairy print on the window.

"It looked similar to a human but it was . . . just too large," she said. "And I'm thinking, 'Oh my God, this creature has opened my door.'"

Chapter Three
BIGFOOT AROUND THE WORLD

ARE THEY ALL THE SAME SPECIES?

People all around the world have seen creatures whose description more or less matches that of Bigfoot. Eyewitness accounts of a hair-covered wild man can be found on every continent except Antarctica, according to a book by famous bigfoot hunter Ivan Sanderson, *Abominable Snowmen: Legend Come to Life.* These wild men are called many different things— sasquatch, skunk ape, yeti, yowie—but could they possibly be the same animal?

There are many similarities between these hidden creatures, from the way they look and behave to the strange sounds they make. Without examples of the creatures, though, it's hard to say whether and how they might be related, and when they went from one species to two or more.

Remember the coelacanth? That's the fish everyone thought was extinct until 1938. The other variety of this living fossil is a *separate species*. The two split apart from each other millions of years ago, according to a doctoral student at the University of California– Berkeley who examined the DNA in tissues from the Indonesian and Indian Ocean varieties. They're related—just not the same creature, which is why they have different names.

At this point, we can't know whether the various wild man creatures spotted around the world might be related, or whether they are related to apes or hominids (human relatives who walk on two feet). The best thing to do is continue to make observations and learn as much as we can about animals and their classifications in general.

HOW LIVING THINGS ARE ORGANIZED

You've probably heard the word *species* before. To be of the same species, two individuals have to share enough characteristics to breed offspring. So, two dogs (even if they are different breeds) are members of the same species. They can have puppies! Hooray! But a dog and a cat, alas, cannot.

There are some tricky exceptions to this. For example, a female horse and a male donkey can produce an offspring called a mule, even though they are different species with a different number of chromosomes. Generally, mules can't reproduce, and hybrids that can't reproduce can't be classified as a species. (Less well-known is the hinny, which comes from a male horse and a female donkey.)

But it's not all about breeding. Species can also be defined based on their DNA, their internal and external physical characteristics (called "morphology"), and their "ecological niche," which depends on where it lives, what it eats, and how it behaves to survive.

So there's actually quite a lot of information you need to have to determine exactly what species an animal belongs to, and even with known animals, researchers sometimes make observations that lead them to reclassify animals. For example, as recently as 2012, a group of Western chimpanzees have been observed hunting with spears, living in caves, and playing in water—things so un-chimp-like, some experts are wondering whether they're another species.

What's more, species is just one level of the organizational system scientists use to understand the relationships living things have to one another. It's entirely possible that bigfoot, yetis, and other wild man creatures are as distinct from one another as humans are from chimpanzees.

WHAT GROUPS WOULD BIGFOOT FIT INTO?

The organization system starts with "kingdom," which includes all animals. Each category below divides animals further into groups (and there's a separate system for plants).

Kingdom: All animals.

Phylum: *Chordata*. Bigfoot, great apes, and human beings (*Homo sapiens sapiens*) would be in this group together.

Class: *Mammalia*. Bigfoot, humans, and the great apes are also mammals.

Order: *Primate*. Bigfoot, humans, and the great apes are also primates.

Family: *Hominidae*. Humans and the great apes are all in the same family. Bigfoot would most likely be classified here.

Genus: Human beings are in the genus *Homo*. The apes split off here into different groups. Would bigfoot? We don't know.

Species: Humans are *sapiens* (which means "wise"). The apes, meanwhile, split further into species (and some into subspecies).

Memory Trick

You can remember the classification categories with this handy sentence: Kings Play Chess On Fridays, Generally Speaking.

While we don't know exactly where a bigfoot would fit in the system, it's reasonable to assume we'd share classifications all the way down to the genus level, which is where we split from apes. Humans are the only species left with the *Homo* genus, although others, including *Homo neanderthalensis*, *Homo erectus*, and *Homo habilis*, once walked the planet. And remember that bit about donkeys and horses sometimes producing offspring? *Homo sapiens sapiens* and *Homo neanderthalensis* did just this, which shows why the "what's a species" question can sometimes require a long answer. According to a paper written by a Swedish evolutionary biologist named Svante Pääbo, everyone who is not of African descent has a tiny bit of Neanderthal DNA—between one and four percent. Wherever bigfoot might fit in, it's reasonable to assume that there could be separate species of bigfoot—yetis, orang pendeks, and so on—just as there are two species of gorilla (plus a number of subspecies). The bigger question, and one we can't answer without an actual bigfoot to study, is whether the creature is an ape or a hominid.

Based on suspected bigfoot footprints that have been collected, we do know its footprints aren't ape-like. Apes have thumb-like toes. But bigfoot tracks are also unlike human ones—they are broader and have longer heels and toes, no arches, and a more flexible mid-foot (see Chapter 8).

Interestingly, their toe length as a percentage of the overall foot length compares with *Australopithecus afarensis*, an early bipedal hominid, according to Jeff Meldrum, author of *Sasquatch: Legend Meets Science,* and an expert in anatomy and walking and the evolution of feet. So at least in this regard, bigfoot has feet more like a hominid's than an ape's, which is fascinating because scientists believe all other hominids besides humans—*Homo sapiens*—are extinct. If it turns out bigfoot is a hominid that only looked extinct, like the coelacanth, a lot of textbooks will have to be rewritten.

SPOTTED!

"I Dare You to Look Out the Window"

Mark Stanislawski's family had a rabbit at their Oregon campground they always figured attracted bigfoot. Some time later, he and a couple of friends thought they'd do a little experiment to lure a sasquatch closer.

They might have gotten more than they bargained for.

They hung a cage six feet above the ground, suspending the rabbit inside. Then they put a glow stick on its cage, knowing that if anything passed, they'd be able to see it.

"I'm looking out the window and I seen him pass through the camp," Mark said. "And so I told my friend Steve here, 'I dare you to look out the window.'"

Steve did. The rabbit was going nuts, running around really fast in the cage, "like something's out there."

And then he saw it—a huge hand slowly move in front of the cage. The next morning, when they went back, they found tracks. Another friend who was in the Bigfoot Field Researchers Organization showed them how to make a cast and how to measure the length of the stride using a piece of fishing line.

Whatever had scared the rabbit during the night had a fifty-three-inch stride. Just like a bigfoot's.

HOW DO LIVING THINGS EVOLVE?

So how is it that species change and turn into different organisms, anyway? Evolution. Over time, living things change. This happens across generations, not within them—a really important thing to keep in mind. Some people dismiss evolution because they find it hard to believe that monkeys can turn into people. This sort of monkey business doesn't happen, of course. But over time, changes in living things *do* occur.

All sorts of things can bring these changes about. Changes in climate can mean certain characteristics give a survival advantage, whether that characteristic is size, color, ability to metabolize certain foods, or any number of things. Over time, characteristics that are disadvantageous will disappear, because the animals that have it don't survive to reproduce and pass the traits along.

Sometimes environmental changes can be abrupt. Let's say something permanently separates one group of animals from another. This happened in 1995 to a group of fifteen iguanas that rode out Hurricane Marilyn by floating on top of uprooted trees until they reached Anguilla, an island in the Caribbean. Over time, if these iguanas survive, they might adapt to the climate on their new home. Iguanas that are especially well suited to the environment—let's say they're a nicely disguised color—might have more offspring, passing along the traits that served them well as they reproduce. After a number of generations, they might change enough so that they look like a new species.

And of course, sometimes these changes are gradual. Over a very long time, the continents move apart or land bridges might be covered by water. What once was a single species of animals might over many generations develop enough differences between them that they become two species.

ABOMINABLE SNOWMAN

The abominable snowman didn't always have such an exciting name. British explorers who said they spotted him in Tibet called him a wild man. And the natives had their own names for the creature. You might have heard the Nepalese name, *yeti*. This isn't a specific name for one animal, though. It's kind of like the word "bird," which can refer to ducks and eagles and pigeons and all sorts of things (or monster, which might mean a werewolf, vampire, wendigo, or zombie).

There are three basic types of yeti:
- A big, ferocious, bear-like "*dzuteh-a*"
- A small, monkeyish wild man called "*the-lma*"
- A half human, half animal called "*met-teh*"

As a human-like animal, the meh-teh sounds most like the Himalayan version of bigfoot. Bigfoot scholars believe the first time the creature was mentioned in print was in 1832. An Englishman named B. H. Hodgson lived in the court of Nepal and heard stories from native hunters about a furry, tailless demon who walked on two feet. At the time, the sensible Hodgson thought it was probably an orangutan.

Almost sixty years later, in 1889, a lieutenant-colonel and surgeon in the British Army named L. A. Waddell happened upon mysterious tracks in northwest Sikkim. He thought they belonged to the yeti.

Then, in 1900, we had the first Westerner's sighting of a yeti. William Hugh Knight, a member of the Royal Society Club, a sort of scientific advisory board, described the creature he saw as just under six feet tall, "stark naked in the bitter cold," and kind of pale yellow with matted hair on its head, a bit on its face, splayed feet and huge hands.

All of this is classic bigfoot evidence: stories from natives, footprints, sightings. And yet none of it was absolute proof.

Two decades passed and Westerners began to look at Mount Everest, the world's tallest mountain, as an irresistible challenge. In 1921, Lieutenant Colonel C. K. Howard-Bury was in charge of a mission to scout a path to the mighty mountain. On Lhakpa La, a Tibetan mountain pass almost four miles above sea level, they found something totally unexpected: tracks that seemed human.

Howard-Bury had native porters with him. These people thought right away that the tracks must belong to the wild man of the snows. Howard-Bury, more of a stuffy British sort, thought such talk was poppycock, the sort of bogeyman story your mom and dad might tell you to scare you into your best behavior. He figured the tracks were wolf prints that had been

stepped on more than once, making them look larger and like something else. But he did send word of the discovery to a newspaper columnist.

This is where the abominable snowman accidentally got its name. Howard-Bury told the columnist that the track belonged to what the natives called a *metoh kangmi*. A *kangmi* is a "snow man." *Metoh* means "wild man," so the words together translate as "wild man of the snow."

But the columnist, a man named Henry Newman, messed up the words. Instead of *metoh*, he translated the word *metch*, which means "filthy" in Tibetan. He dubbed the creature that made the tracks the "abominable snowman," which was so intriguing that word spread from Tibet to India to England and then to the United States, as newspapers picked it up (that's how things went viral before there was the Internet).

People really started to wonder what was up there on that snowy peak. Interest in climbing Mount Everest stayed strong. But it took many years before anyone succeeded. In 1951, a famous British climber named Eric Shipton was trying to find a path that led to the mountaintop. As they crossed an icefall to the head of the Menlung Glacier through knee-deep snow untouched by human feet, Shipton found something strange.

"Where the snow covering the ice was thin . . . was a well-preserved impression of the creature's foot." The print had three wide toes and a broad thumb. Shipton's team followed the prints across a crevasse, a deep crack in a glacier. It looked as though the creature had jumped and used its toes to grip onto the other side, he wrote.

Curious, the climbers followed the footprints for about a mile before they lost them. Shipton took pictures, using his boot and an ice pick to show the scale of these strange tracks. The experience was sort of a creepy one. It gave him the feeling that the creature was lurking "somewhere in the moonlit silence."

When Shipton wrote about his trip for the London *Times*, which printed a photo in the Dec. 7, 1951, edition, people were intrigued. Many other publications wrote articles and Hollywood made movies (including *The Abominable Snowman of the Himalayas)*. No one was quite sure what it was. Britain's Natural History Museum theorized langurs—long-tailed Asian monkeys—had left the tracks. Others said they might have been left by monks wearing snowshoes (or no shoes). An anthropologist at Johns-Hopkins University, William Straus, guessed it was a Himalayan red bear, but a biologist named Lawrence Swan countered that those animals are only in the eastern Himalayas, where these tracks were laid in the west.

One name of the Himalayan chain—Mahalangur Himal—is intriguing. It means mountains (himal) of the great apes (langur). Was the truth of the presence of giant apes on the remote, snowy peak hidden in the name of the mountain range itself?

The Himalayan red bear

ABOMINABLE SNOWMAN TRACKS DEBUNKED?

After he climbed Mount Everest in 1953, Edmund Hillary was a star. He was also curious about the yeti said to live on the mountain he'd conquered. It made a good deal of sense to him, now that he'd mastered the world's largest mountain, to go in search of its most mysterious inhabitant. In a *New York Times Magazine* article, he said, "I believe there is sufficient evidence to warrant a closer search for the maker of these tracks."

So, in 1960, he set out to see whether he might find the creature. The expedition was serious and well funded, with twenty-two scientists and mountaineers, six Sherpas, one hundred fifty porters, and even a journalist named Desmond Doig, who later created a comic strip called *Bing: The Abominable Snow-Baby.*

They left Katmandu, Nepal, on September 13, 1960, in search of tracks and other evidence. When they returned home, they were convinced the yeti did not exist.

What happened?

It was a number of things. First, remember those strange, long tracks Eric Shipton saw?

They figured out a scientific explanation for them. At high altitudes, it's very cold and snow doesn't melt. Instead, it goes straight from a solid form to water vapor. This is called sublimation.

When an animal makes a footprint in the snow, part of the print might be exposed to sunlight, while part remains in shadow. The part that sees sunlight sublimates. In doing so, it gets longer and wider. If only part of the print is exposed to sunlight, it will stretch unevenly, looking like a different sort of print. But because there is no melting, the edges stay crisp, making the track look freshly laid.

One big clue for the team was that the tracks in a particular area always faced the same direction. The Sherpas had an explanation for this—that the yeti could turn its feet around to fool anyone who might be following it. But this explanation is complicated and sounds a bit made-up. It also depends on some unusual feet. Sublimation

is a simpler explanation that works and can be demonstrated.

Occam's razor is a scientific principle that says the best explanation for something is the one that requires the fewest assumptions. Scientists are fond of this principle. It helps them create good hypotheses—educated guesses about something—and then devise experiments that let them test whether their guesses are true. This methodical process replaces assumptions with patterns and behaviors that can be observed by independent witnesses.

Guessing that a yeti has feet that can swivel around in many directions isn't something that can be observed until we have a yeti on hand, so it can't be tested and proved or disproved until then. But you can make a footprint in the snow in Nepal and watch what happens when the sun hits part of it. Other people can check your work. This gives reliable, trustworthy results.

What's more, Hillary's team considered more than footprints. There were the yeti scalps sometimes displayed in villages. Were they real or not?

The team figured out how to make a serow pelt (that's a goat-antelope native to the region) look like a yeti scalp. It was convincing enough that it even fooled one of the people who worked on the fake. In exchange for renovating a monastery and fund-raising for a school for the locals, the team sent back one of these yeti scalps and a so-called yeti skin for analysis. Scientists matched the skin to the skin and fur of a blue bear, which is a known native of the region. Bristles from the scalp, meanwhile, were found to be from an animal related to the pelt.

With that, Hillary was convinced the yeti was merely a legend, and he was so popular and respected that many people took his word for it, although believers still remained unconvinced and did their best to point out flaws with the research and the expedition.

SPOTTED!
"You Could Hear the Footsteps"

Casey Skodje and Shane Hamre were bow hunting in the dense woods just outside of Yacolt in southwest Washington State, prime Bigfoot country.

"On the way in, we kept hearing random noises," Shane said. "It started off like sticks breaking every once in a while." The noises got louder over time. "I could hear something physically walking."

His buddy Casey said, "You could hear it brushing through the bushes, but you could hear the footsteps, too."

Shane turned around and walked backward, pointing his gun into the darkness of the woods. He yelled at it. "If you're a person, you better identify yourself, otherwise you're gonna get shot!"

No one said a word. From the evidence, Cliff theorizes that they were being escorted out of the area by none other than a sasquatch.

SASQUATCH

Canadian folklore is full of stories of wild men. Very often, these creatures were nocturnal and hairy (but not always). Sometimes, they stole young women away. Other times, they helped young men who'd been cast out. Some could speak. Some could only whistle. Strangely, some had spiked toes or legs that wouldn't bend (which meant they could only run downhill).

In 1929, a Canadian teacher named John Burns wrote

a story about these creatures for the magazine *Maclean's*. He named the creature sasquatch, and he helped form a consistent image for the furry monster out of folklore. Many of the details are consistent with aspects the *Finding Bigfoot* team hears from people describing their own encounters with squatches:

- *They're about eight feet tall;*
- *They're covered with dark hair;*
- *They're uncivilized;* and
- *They throw rocks.*

A few details, though, aren't commonly reported but still made it into his article:

- *They can speak and have magical powers;* and
- *They covet women (Burns told one story of a woman who was abducted by a sasquatch and then gave birth to a baby who died a few hours later).*

In 1941, a First Nations woman named Jeannie Chapman lived in Ruby Creek with her family. One day her child told her a big cow was coming, so she glanced out the window. What she saw was no cow. As soon as the creature worked its way into their storage shed, she took her children and fled to the Ruby Creek station. Chapman's husband and other men found footprints and a broken barrel of salted salmon when they checked out the scene. The Bellingham, Washington, sheriff's station investigated and opened a file on the case. Coincidentally, Burns covered the sighting as a journalist—but he thought it was a bear.

Years later, a newspaper owner named John Green was aware of sasquatch, but chalked it up to legend. Then he met a man named René Dahinden in 1956. Dahinden had heard of the yeti in Nepal and hoped to find the Canadian equivalent. The next year proved to be a turning point. The town of Harrison Hot Springs offered $600 for a civic project to help celebrate its centennial. Someone proposed a sasquatch hunt. They rejected the idea and bought a furnace for the new community hall (adults can be so boring), but people went nuts about the sasquatch idea.

Pretty soon, Green figured out that local people really did take the creature seriously, and it appealed to his curiosity as a journalist to find out more. He brought evidence he found to a zoologist at Provincial Museum, and eventually hired Dahinden to be a reporter on his newspaper staff.

Over the years, Green branched out his research to include bigfoot, interviewing people who'd claimed they had sightings, including Albert Ostman, a retired logger who said he'd been taken captive and lived with a sasquatch family for days before he used a can of snuff to make a wily escape. Green also wrote several books and followed the trail of bigfoot for decades without giving up.

BIGFOOT

There are more bigfoots hidden in the forests of North America than there are pandas in the wild, according to estimates of the Bigfoot Field Researchers Organization, which estimates there are 2,000 to 6,000 of the hairy creatures roaming free.

Bigfoot folklore is old. The Hoopa Indians, who live on a reservation near Humboldt County, tell tales of giant wild men, "creek devils" and "O-mah," which are huge, hairy, smelly monsters. There are also ancient cave paintings (see page 15). And a Pacific Northwest tribe called the Tsimshian [CHIM-she-un] has carved stone sculptures depicting ape-like creatures. This is stunning, given North America has no native apes. It's hard to imagine what might have inspired the artwork if there wasn't some creature Native Americans had seen.

But bigfoot didn't really become big, so to speak, until 1958.

That was the year a logging company worker in northern California named Jerry Crew, who was by all accounts reliable, hard-working, and religious, hopped on his bulldozer for another day's

When does bigfoot have a capital B?

The creature whose footprints Jerry Crew found in 1958 is the one that inspired the name Bigfoot. When you're talking about this particular animal, you use a capital letter. When you're talking about bigfoot as a species, you use a little "b."

work when he found big, man-like footprints all around him. It was late summer, August 27, to be exact. He found more tracks in September and took his evidence to a taxidermist who said he could capture better detail if he took a casting of the print. So Crew did just that and brought back a sixteen-inch track.

A newspaper columnist from the *Humboldt Times*, Andrew Genzoli, was curious. He'd received a letter about the tracks and, one day when he had a bit of extra space in his column, he ran the letter. A reporter on the newspaper staff, Betty Allen, started writing news articles about the mysterious find. Then, in October, Genzoli met with Crew, who had his picture taken with the cast for the paper.

Genzoli called the creature Bigfoot, and he wrote about its effect on the road crew. "The men are often convinced that they are being watched. However, they believe it is not an unfriendly watching." Rather, the creature was more of an invisible

That's one big footprint.

supervisor, stopping by daily to inspect their work. They measured the space between footprints, and Genzoli wrote that Bigfoot appeared to have a fifty-inch stride that stretched to ten feet as it ran.

His column was a sensation. Genzoli got more than 2,500 letters. A game show called *Truth or Consequences* offered a thousand-dollar reward to anyone who could explain the origin of the tracks. People wondered if it was an ape. Or a bear. Swedish people with large feet. A race of giants living in the mountains (this rumor got pretty wild—these giants were said to be lost relatives of the Atlanteans).

All along, Jerry Crew believed they were real, even as newspapers duked it out with one another. One of Crew's bosses, Ray Wallace, even threatened to sue anyone who called the tracks a hoax. But here's the surprising part. After Wallace died in 2002, his son said Wallace had made the tracks himself. When Wallace's obituary ran in *The Seattle Times*, it even contained the quote "Bigfoot is dead."

Was it Wallace all along? Bigfooters were convinced the tracks were real. John Green, the Canadian newspaper editor who studied sasquatch for much of his career, drove two thousand miles to California to see what the big deal was. His map was unreliable and he got lost, and the roads were dusty, but his journey was successful in one regard because he found tracks. Looking at them was remarkable, he wrote.

"I had never expected there would be anything to see." He was glad his wife was there with him because it helped her be understanding as he endured this decades-long quest. He thought the tracks he'd found were genuine, and noted their similarity to the ones from the Ruby Creek incident so many years earlier. How could separate people faking both sets of tracks manage to come up with something so similar?

Meanwhile, members of the Bigfoot Field Researchers Organization carry on the work, but with the advantages of modern technology. The group has a database with thousands of bigfoot sightings submitted by users. The sightings paint a picture of a hairy, nocturnal animal that ranges between seven and ten feet tall, weighs around six hundred fifty pounds, and has flat feet and body odor.

SKUNK APE

Far from the Pacific Northwest, in the opposite corner of the country, in an entirely different sort of environment, lives the skunk ape. This devastatingly smelly, seven-foot-tall hairy creature resides in the boggy places in Florida, Louisiana, and eastern Texas, where more than a million and a half acres of impenetrable forests and swamps provide these elusive beasts with plenty of privacy and protein.

"The edges of the canals in Florida provide a number of food resources for skunk apes," Matt Moneymaker says. "There are fish and reptiles and birds, and these canals run for miles like highways across the Everglades."

But that's not all that's on a skunk ape menu. They're also believed to eat deer, wild hogs, alligators, and even swamp apples, Moneymaker says. "That's how they're able to survive in such an unforgiving environment."

ARE SKUNK APES BIGFOOTS?
OR A SEPARATE ANIMAL?

This isn't something that can be determined without specimens of each creature. Like bigfoot, the skunk ape is hairy, but has been described as smaller, with more hair that is lighter in color, sort of a reddish black, according to the Skunk Ape Research Headquarters in Ochopee, Florida. The headquarters also reports that male skunk apes are six to seven feet tall, weighing in at more than four hundred fifty pounds—so, large, but not bigfoot big. Females, meanwhile, run five to six feet tall and weigh up to two hundred fifty pounds.

As with bigfoots and yetis, stories of skunk apes stretch back in time, often before white explorers arrived. The Miccosukee Seminole nation in southern Florida tell stories of a tall, hairy man. And the first newspaper reference dates back to 1850 in a story about a wild man covered in hair spotted by Arkansas farmers. Since then there have been a couple of notable sightings: one in 1977 in which the man who had the encounter described its stench.

"It stunk awful," Charlie Stoeckman said. "Like a dog that hasn't been bathed in a year and suddenly gets rained on."

In another notable encounter that happened in 2000, a man driving near Trout, Louisiana, claimed to have hit a man in a fur coat with his car . . . but they never found the victim. For sure he hit something, though. His car was badly damaged.

Witnesses have described the odor of a skunk ape as rotten eggy. Some theorize that these creatures hide in alligator dens, absorbing the smell of swamp gas or rotting animals. Skunk apes no doubt sweat in the hot Florida weather. And, says Dave Shealy, who runs the Skunk Ape Research Center with his brother Jack, skunk apes don't bathe.

SKUNK APE BAIT

The Skunk Ape Research Headquarters has a warning for those of you who'd put out bait trying to catch a specimen: reconsider. The more bait you put out for these rare creatures, the less likely they are to be able to feed themselves. What's more, leaving food on the side of the road makes it more likely they will be hit by cars. It's also not legal to do in national parks or state-owned preserves.

If you have permission from a private property owner to leave out a little skunk ape bait, though, dry beans make the best bait, followed by deer liver, and then corn, rice, or dog food.

If you opt for deer liver, make sure you keep it safe by keeping it cold until you've chosen a bait site, and only put out bait if you've spotted a skunk ape and want to lure it. Otherwise, you're just feeding buzzards, which love the stuff.

If you opt for dry beans, lima beans are the most popular choice. Making sure you choose a dry spot (because moisture will rot the beans), clear a ten-foot-square area with a rake. Cover it evenly with a pound of large, dry lima beans.

You can use wet beans, too. Prepare these by soaking a pound of beans overnight in eight cups of water. Then dump the pile in the center of the ten-foot area that you've cleared of debris, or hang it in a pot from a tree limb in the middle of this same space.

The sour smell of the wet beans is believed to be appealing to skunk apes. After five days or so, you have to remove your wet beans.

And if a skunk ape takes the bait, keep it quiet. This will protect the animal from unscrupulous sorts who might want to come in and shoot the creature.

Mmm . . . skunk ape bait!

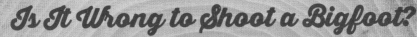

Is It Wrong to Shoot a Bigfoot?

The only definitive proof of a bigfoot, sasquatch, skunk ape, or yeti is an actual animal to study. While bigfoot searchers have gathered many footprints and other examples of evidence, science requires an actual animal or part thereof to be officially declared a species. What if the only way to prove bigfoot exists is to kill it? Some bigfoot seekers over the years have argued that this approach is ethical. It's worth sacrificing one to prove the animal exists. Others think it's a terrible idea to kill such a rare creature. Doing so could put an already rare species at risk. In considering your own answer to this question, think about how you'd feel if you purposely killed the last animal of its kind on the planet. Would it be worth it to prove one existed—only to make it disappear forever?

SHOOT A BIGFOOT, GO TO JAIL?

In Skamania County, Washington, an ordinance passed in 1969 makes it illegal to kill a bigfoot. Anyone who hunted bigfoot and committed a "willful and wanton slaying" could be convicted of a felony, fined up to $10,000, and sent to jail for up to five years. The law was softened a bit in 1984. Now, bigfoot hunting is a gross misdemeanor punishable with a $1,000 fine and up to a year in the clink.

In 2012, a bigfooter in New York tried to get the state's Department of Environmental Conservation to pass a similar no-hunting law, but the state declined, saying "no program or action in relation to mythical animals is warranted."

SPOTTED!

"It Just Ripped up There So Quick"

Northern California's Humboldt County is a Bigfoot hotbed, but is most famous for being the location where Roger Patterson and Bob Gimlin filmed "Patty," believed to be a female Bigfoot walking by Bluff Creek in the Six Rivers region.

Serene White had a similar encounter one afternoon.

Dead battery, she thought. She'd left the music on in her boom box. No big deal. She'd go back up to the top of the road and meet her uncle with a charger.

As she walked back down to the river, a friend who was with her said, "Hey, do you hear that?"

It sounded like something drinking. And then, quick as a flash, whatever it was took off. "It just ripped up there so quick," she said, pointing to the hillside on the riverbank. It passed through a wall of thicket like it was nothing. "I remember being freaked out because if that thing can go up there that quick, how quick could it get to me?"

She's seen bear and deer before, and neither could travel that swiftly. What's more, neither came close to the size of the mystery creature.

"It was huge," she said. With the *Finding Bigfoot* team, she estimated its size to be nine feet tall.

What could it possibly have been?

"I think Serene saw a sasquatch," Matt Moneymaker said.

GIGANTOPITHECUS

Fossils form only when conditions are just right—most living things die and decay without a trace. But when an animal dies in a way that allows its bones to be replaced with minerals over a period of time, it turns into a fossil. This can happen when a body is buried in sediment and covered with seawater, when it's entombed without oxygen, and when there's not too much heat or pressure put on it.

The fossil record isn't complete by any stretch. Some experts estimate we might only have five percent of primate species that made it through this process. Another way of looking at it: We have no record of most animals that have walked the planet. This also means there are a lot of possible bigfoot ancestors that we don't know about.

One of the rare possibilities we do know about is Gigantopithecus, a primate species that might have gone unrecognized except for a bit of luck on the part of a paleontologist named Ralph von Koenigswald. In 1935, he was in China searching for dragon bones, which is what the Chinese believed the fossilized teeth and bones of long-vanished animals to be. He came back with something cooler than a dragon bone: a massive ape tooth. The thing was stunning, twice as big as a gorilla's tooth. He named it *Gigantopithecus blacki*.

Then, in 1950, an Italian expedition to China found an entire Gigantopithecus jawbone. Findings of this humongous ape are rare, and the only proof we have that such a massive ape once lived. In all, there are just a few jaws (and hundreds of single teeth).

It would be really nice to have a skull or even a full skeleton. But by observing the shapes of the teeth and quality of the enamel, which were similar to early hominids that walked upright on two feet, scientists can use Zadig's method to guess what these creatures might have been like and what they ate. They theorize these creatures were nine-foot-tall apes that—according to the fossil record—disappeared from the planet about 100,000 years ago. This means they were alive at the same time as *Homo sapiens sapiens* (that's human beings to you and me).

With the limited fossil evidence, it's hard to tell how the Gigantopithecus might have traveled around—on all fours or on two feet. This is the sort of thing you can tell by looking at a skull or the bones of a pelvis, legs, knee joints, and foot

bones, none of which we have at this point. But in all likelihood, it was too big to swing from the trees. It either walked on two or four legs.

The leading bigfoot expert, Jeffrey Meldrum, a professor of anatomy and anthropology at Idaho State University, believes it's possible bigfoot

Average-sized monkey skull. The Gigantopithecus would be much larger!

is some form of Gigantopithecus that made its way from East Asia on a land bridge that every so often linked Asia and North America. Humans managed to cross the sea this way. And if Sasquatch or its ancestors made it to North America this way, it would also explain in part why there isn't a fossil record that shows the emergence of giant apes. If they didn't evolve in North America but instead traveled there, you wouldn't find ancestor species. Also, its giant body and thick tooth enamel might have equipped it to survive in the colder north.

MORE PUZZLE PIECES THAT FIT

The sasquatch's supersize also makes sense from a scientific standpoint, Meldrum has argued. Other animals living closer to poles are bigger than their relatives in tropical climates. Polar bears, for example, can weigh almost 1,500 pounds. But the spectacled bear found in tropical South America tops out at around 300 pounds.

This is called Bergmann's rule, by the way— the tendency of animals living in the north to be

bigger. Being big helps them hold on to body heat better. It also gives them more room for big bellies, which house the kind of intestines an animal needs to break down the coarser food in northern latitudes.

What's more, Gigantopithecus isn't the only ape that might be linked to sasquatch. Meldrum wrote in his book, *Sasquatch: Legend Meets Science*, that the Miocene era (about twenty-three million

to about five million years ago) offered a huge variety of the apes.

"For a time, Earth truly was 'a planet of the apes,'" he said.

What if the descendants of those apes are alive today, living in stealth in the wilderness? It's not a totally oddball idea. Remember the coelacanth. Everyone thought this fish had been gone for millions of years when someone found a living example.

THE YOWIE

In the late 1700s in Australia, early white settlers thought the Aborigines were trying to scare them off with tales of a "Narcoonah," a wild man living in the forests. But then, in 1790, newspapers carried reports of the first yowie sighting by a white man in a small town that is now known as Sydney. During the next century, this sort of thing happened more frequently, and from all around the vast continent.

The creatures have been described as intelligent, smelly, broad-shouldered, and powerfully built upright walkers that weigh between five hundred and eight hundred pounds, and as with the North American bigfoot, are believed to be nocturnal omnivores. Witnesses have seen them swiping chicken and other livestock, as well as fruit, road kill, and garbage.

They're also reclusive, but signs of their presence might include snapped and bent trees, trails, and strangely woven branches.

A BIGFOOT BY ANY OTHER NAME

One of the most compelling things about bigfoot is that people all around the world tell similar stories about the creature. If bigfoot doesn't exist, how do you explain these stories? Of course, not everyone calls the creature bigfoot or sasquatch, two names we're most familiar with.

Here are a few of the many other names that have been used to describe bigfoot-like creatures.

Wild man: China
The Alma: Mongolia
Metoh-Kangmi: Tibet
Snow Person, Forest Creature: Russia
Ba'oosh: Tsimshian (CHIM-she-un) tribe of the Pacific Northwest
Chie-tanka: Lakota or Western Sioux
Chiha-tanka: Dakota or Eastern Sioux
Rugaru: Turtle Mountain Ojibwa nation in North Dakota
S-cwene'y'ti: Colville Indians

Orang Pendek: Indonesia
Yeren: China
Woodbooger/Beast of Gum Hill: southwest Virginia
Kushtaka, also known among the Tlingit people as Water Devil because the creature was often seen near the water hunting fish
Knobby: a creature in the Carpenter's Knob area of North Carolina
La Llorona: Louisiana (the word is Spanish for "crying woman")

TIMELINE:
BIGFOOT, YETI, AND SASQUATCH

500–1,000 years ago: Bigfoot pictograms made in Painted Rock

1832: Englishman B. H. Hodgson reports native Nepalese hunters are talking about a furry, tailless demon that walks on two feet.

July 4, 1884: A young sasquatch dubbed "Jacko" is captured on the Fraser River in Vancouver. A newspaper reports it (but the story dies out there).

1889: Lieutenant-Colonel L. A. Waddell sees mysterious footprints in Himalaya.

1896: Del Norte County newspaper article describes a wild man that was about seven feet high, with a bulldog head, short ears, and long hair. This wild man had a shrill soprano voice that sounded like a terrified woman.

1924: A miner named Fred Beck reports that apes armed with rocks had attacked his camp. The *Portland Oregonian* carries a news story about it. Beck claims to have shot the creature.)

1924: Albert Ostman claims to have been kidnapped by a family of sasquatches (he signed an affidavit in 1957 swearing it was true).

1929: John Burns writes an article about sasquatches for a Canadian magazine.

1935: Ralph von Koenigswald finds a Gigantopithecus tooth in China.

1941: Jeannie Chapman sees a sasquatch outside her home in Ruby Creek, British Columbia.

Nov. 8, 1951: Mountain climber Eric Shipton photographs what appears to be yeti tracks on the Menlung Glacier in the Himalayas.

1955: A highway worker named William Roe wanders into the mountains on a break and meets a shapely female sasquatch who was stripping leaves from a branch with her teeth. He follows a trail of her poop to her nest, but decides she looks too human to shoot.

1958: Jerry Crew finds Bigfoot tracks.

August 28, 1967: Journalist John Green gets a call about fresh bigfoot tracks; a cultural anthropologist views the tracks and is the first representative of a scientific institution in North America sent to study tracks.

October 20, 1967: Patterson-Gimlin shoots footage of what appears to be a female bigfoot walking along Bluff Creek in Humboldt County, California.

April 1, 1969: Skamania County, Washington, makes it illegal to kill a bigfoot there after a sighting.

September 22, 2000: A suspected bigfoot body print is found in the Skookum Meadow area of Washington State's Gifford Pinchot Forest.

February 11, 2012: London Trackway is discovered in Oregon.

BIGFOOT WITNESS PHOTO

Chapter Four
HOME SMELLY HOME

HOW TO SPOT A BIGFOOT DWELLING

*If the people are away, they always
know when [bigfoots] are coming
very near by their strong smell,
which is most intolerable.*

—A letter from Rev. Elkanah Walker to the American Board
of Commissioners for Foreign Missions, 1840

The more you know about an animal—what it eats, how it travels, where it's likely to live—the better chance you have of finding a sample of one. This is why bigfoot researchers have pondered where a sasquatch sleeps at night.

In a cave? In a hole? In hollow trees? Certainly all are possible.

But to get to the best possible answer for this question, some bigfoot researchers have turned to the gorilla for clues. Along with bonobos, chimpanzees, and orangutans, gorillas are great apes. They're not as big as bigfoot. They don't walk on two feet (at least not most of the time). But they are a large, hairy primate that

has managed to elude scientists for many years. Their behavior and sleeping habits could provide valuable clues in the hunt for bigfoot.

Gorillas sleep in nests. When they choose an area to bed down, one of the criteria they use is whether it has enough material for them to make their beds. And while there isn't a single method of building a gorilla nest, they usually take bent and broken vines, twigs, leaves, and branches to form an individual sleeping area (although baby gorillas share one with their mamas for the first three or so years). The nest keeps the gorilla off the ground and provides a bit of safety as they sleep by making them

less likely to tumble out of a tree or down a slope as they doze.

They build nests at least once a day, in part because they move around looking for vegetation to eat. If they stayed in one place, they'd literally eat themselves out of house and home. Another reason they might move, though, is that fresh bedding makes it less likely parasites will have a chance to set up shop.

The adults in the gorilla troop build their first nest of the day after their morning's foraged meal. (The kids get to play.) They nap in these nests, wake up for more eating, and then build a new nest for nighttime, never using the same nest twice. Gorilla researchers love finding nests of gorilla troops, because they can tell all sorts of information about the animals—how many, what they're doing—just from this single set of clues.

The same goes for bigfooters. They keep their eyes peeled for sleeping quarters—for clumps of sticks and branches that appear to have been twisted off and arranged in such a way that a sasquatch would have a soft, protected place to sleep, even if it's just used once.

CLOSE-UP: A BIGFOOT NEST AND HOW IT WAS MADE

In 2001, what some believe are three bigfoot nests in various stages of construction were found on private property near Sonora, California. Two nests were unfinished, but one looked as though it had been recently used, according to Kathy Moskowitz Strain, an anthropologist and USDA forest worker, who found the site and wrote an article about it for the Bigfoot Field Researchers Organization.

According to her report, the nests were in an

area with plenty of water and vegetation, including black oak, interior live oak, Jeffrey pine, manzanita, and bracken fern. The area also had a stream that was a tributary of the Stanislaus River, as well as a native deer herd, which meant plenty of food and water.

According to the USDA Forest Service records, there are no identified Native American sites and the area is not used for recreation. In other words, it's decent sasquatch territory: private and graced with food and water. Only its proximity to people makes it somewhat less desirable, Moskowitz said.

Moskowitz also found fresh, fourteen-inch Bigfoot tracks nearby, and the three nests were built near one another. The complete one was 1.3 meters high, 1.6 meters wide, and 1.9 meters long, and was made from live oak and Jeffrey pine. Its doorway opened to the northwest. The "padding" inside appeared matted from recent use.

Moskowitz waited a few months to be sure the nest was abandoned, and measured a 213-by-30-centimeter body imprint in it. She also took it apart to understand how it had been made. It looked as though a twelve-foot live oak tree had been bent over and secured with a heavy rock to create a dome. Then, fifteen Jeffrey pine branches, each an average of seven feet long, were stripped of smaller limbs and woven into the branches of the bent oak. Holes were filled in with smaller sticks. Then the interior was padded in three layers. The top was made of three centimeters of fresh moss, bracken ferns, and oak leaves. Below that came four centimeters of dead and decaying leaves. The bottom three centimeters were old moss, bracken fern fronts, and soil.

"Overall, the nest had a spongy, soft consistency," she wrote in her report.

"None of the layers had any apparent smell, other than that of dead and decaying organic material. No rocks or sticks were noted."

She combed through those layers, hoping to find evidence such as bones, teeth, hairs, and blood, but didn't find anything, and microscopic examination showed plant materials, seeds, and insect casings. She didn't find any direct evidence this was a bigfoot nest, but based on its similarities to other nests reported in books by John Bindernagel and Grover Krantz, the overall evidence suggested a lone sasquatch had built and briefly occupied this little refuge in the woods.

OTHER FAVORITE BIGFOOT HANGOUTS

Some bigfooters theorize the animals live in caves, which helps the creature avoid human detection. For certain, people claim to have had encounters in caves.

"I get excited when I see a cave because I've heard so many reports of people encountering a squatch in a cave," Bobo Fay says. "This is perfect squatch habitat."

There are a few scientific reasons bigfoot seekers think the animals could well be hiding out in caves.

BIG EYES: Many reports of bigfoot say the creature's eyes shine at night. This is common among nocturnal creatures. (See Chapter 6 for more information about eye shine and what causes it.) Bigfoot is also said to have large eyes. As with the giant squid, these large eyes would make for better vision in low light.

BIG SMELL: Caves are wet and dank. A furry animal living in such a spot would stink. (If you've ever gotten a whiff of wet dog, then you can imagine a fraction of the odor a much larger, much dirtier bigfoot might produce.)

STRATEGIC SOUNDS: Bigfoots are said to howl and knock. This might be their version of echolocation—using sound and listening to their echoes to navigate and hunt. Bats, whales, and even some blind humans are known to use this technique.

Matt

SPOTTED!
"You Guys Have Got to Check This Out"

Ben Mills's parents were off on a hike with each other in the Marble Mountain range of Humboldt County, leaving Ben and his brother Scott alone at the campsite. But not for long, Ben said.

The parents hightailed it back to the camp and said, "You guys have got to check this out."

The family set out for a strange sort of hut his parents had discovered. There were strange things about it.

"It looked like there were some claw marks. The limbs themselves were broken. There were no saw marks," Ben said.

Matt Moneymaker says this sounds like a possible Bigfoot nest.

"Bigfooters speculate that sasquatches build these type of nests from materials in the surrounding environment, to both protect themselves from the elements and to hide from humans during the day."

As Ben's dad was capturing video of the structure, Ben saw a little speck walking toward them. Its arms looked abnormally long. Its back appeared hunched, which he first thought was a backpack. But it was so tall.

"Then it disappeared," he said. The whole thing was odd . . . that there was someone there alone, the way the creature moved. After the *Finding Bigfoot* team staged a reenactment, Cliff Barackman was convinced it was no hiker they'd seen. He said, "I see no reason to discount that it's a sasquatch."

A PEEK AT SOME CAVES IN NORTH AMERICA

North America has many large caves. For example, Mammoth Cave in Kentucky is the largest known cave in the world, with more than 390 miles that have been explored. The name really describes it—the next biggest cave we know about is only a quarter the size of Mammoth Cave, which might even have more to it than we've been able to measure. The Green River in Kentucky carved Mammoth Cave over a period of ten million years, and all sorts of interesting critters live there—from eyeless fish to white cave spiders. So why not a bigfoot?

Carlsbad Caverns in New Mexico also took millions of

Mammoth Cave in Kentucky

years to form, and are also so big they haven't been fully explored. They're really cool—there are three different underground levels, a four-thousand-foot-long cavern (called Big Room), and even a natural stone structure that looks like a tumbling waterfall of rock.

In Washington State, near an active volcano named Mount St. Helens, there's also a spectacular cave made from a tube of lava. It's got a very provocative name: Ape Cave. Nearby is Ape Canyon, and bigfoot has been spotted in both places. There was even a fight reported in 1924 between some miners and a family of bigfoots.

But the "Ape" in the place names are not necessarily a Bigfoot reference. Instead, the Mount St. Helens tourist Web site says this name might come from a troop of Boy Scouts who explored it

Mount St. Helens

in the 1950s. They were the Mount St. Helens Apes. It's also possible the area was named for early loggers and foresters, who were sometimes called "brush apes."

That said, if bigfoot ever is definitely found to be living in the area, the maps won't have to be changed, will they?

SPOTTED!
Nobody Messes with Tinman

Rodney "Tinman" Mitchell lives on the Hoopa Reservation, a place long linked to bigfoot.

When he had his encounter with the creature, it was nighttime. The sky was moonless, so it was dark. But he knew something was out there.

"My dogs were barking like crazy," he said. "I shined my light right through here and I heard a big snap."

Not one to put up with trespassers or tomfoolery, he blasted two rounds into the night. Then something huge jumped eight feet out of a tree.

"He jumped right into my light and went down over the hill," Tinman said. "I was so

nervous and shook up that I couldn't even figure out how to get the bullet out of the chamber. And I was, like, just fumbling it."

That's when he realized he needed to get himself back in his house. He figures the creature he saw—no way was it someone in a suit—weighed about four hundred pounds and was around six feet tall.

"I could just see his muscles right through here," Tinman said. "He just looked stocky, you know."

There's one more reason Tinman knows it wasn't a person in a suit.

"Nobody messes around here because they know I'll shoot them," he said. "I mean, it's as simple as that."

WHAT YOU MIGHT FIND (AND SMELL) INSIDE A BIGFOOT NEST

If bigfoots are like gorillas, they do not use their nests for long. Remember, gorillas make two nests a day. If bigfoots follow a similar pattern, we should not expect to find sturdy housing intended to last. Likewise, we shouldn't expect to find much evidence beyond the twisted-off, woven branches and arranged bedding.

Nor should we expect to find any sort of tools or decorations. Apes and some monkeys have been observed using tools, but bigfoot is generally not believed to use tools, although there have been sightings of sasquatches using sticks to dig. The theory about why tools aren't found in suspected bigfoot nests is that these creatures don't need to use tools.

Still, there's one thing you can expect to find in a bigfoot nest: a certain odor. Many people who've encountered bigfoot describe a distinctive aroma, either of feces or rotting meat. And one variety, the skunk ape, is named for its distinctive methane smell—think cow farts.

Branches make great gorilla tools.

HOW TO MAKE A BIGFOOT BED

Bigfoots need sleep, just like you. And according to the people who've dedicated their lives to finding the elusive creature, bigfoots prefer beds. Matt Moneymaker has studied every aspect of the animal's behavior and preferences. It's a detail many people ignore.

"But this is a very important thing for understanding how sasquatch live, where they'll go, what they like, and what they don't like."

He believes a good spot for a bigfoot bed is in a secluded area, where people won't stumble across it.

"A place full of pine needles that's in the sunlight," he says. That's what a squatch will like.

He's even built a sasquatch bed by piling up leaves and sun-dried pine needles until he has a thick, mattress-like construction that gives bigfoot a few insulated inches between its body and the ground. And he thinks it's a pretty comfortable way to sleep. "I'm feeling just right here," he says, feeling his mother-nature mattress. "I can hang here for hours."

Sasquatch Snack Attack:
HOW TO EAT LIKE BIGFOOT AND MAKE YETI SPAGHETTI

WHAT DOES BIGFOOT EAT?

Anything goes at the sasquatch snack bar. Bigfoot is an omnivore, which means both plants and animals are on the menu. In the wooded areas in which they are said to live, they might find everything from nuts and berries to rabbits, crawdads, fish, and deer. "Jacko," the suspected juvenile sasquatch found in British Columbia in 1884, was fed berries and milk.

In setting up bait stations, the *Finding Bigfoot* team has left out apples, bacon, peanut butter, doughnuts, bagels, and . . . gag . . . raw liver.

For fun, you might try packing yourself a Bigfoot lunch to take to school. Assuming you're not allergic to peanut butter (and you aren't planning to eat near anyone who is), you might pack yourself a peanut butter bagel with a sliced apple, a container of blueberries, and a carton of milk.

Bigfoot-Inspired Recipes for You to Cook

You'll work up a big appetite hunting for bigfoot. You can keep your belly full from breakfast until dinner with these delicious recipes that are easy enough for you to make—and something your whole family will enjoy.

Yeti Spaghetti is a creamy, white mountain of pasta flavored with lots of garlic and Parmesan cheese, so you will be good and stinky after eating it.

Yeti Spaghetti

1/2 pound dry fettuccine pasta

3 to 4 tablespoons unsalted butter

1 tablespoon of chopped garlic

2/3 cup finely grated Parmesan cheese

Black pepper

1/2 cup cream

1. Boil a big pot of water. Add a pinch of salt and your dry pasta. (You can use fresh pasta, but if you do, don't drop it in the water until your sauce is cooked.)

2. Melt the butter in a saucepan set over low heat. Cook the garlic for about three minutes. Then stir in the cream. Keep stirring this mix over very low heat (don't let it boil) until your pasta is cooked.

3. When your noodles are done, lift them out of the pot and put them into the sauce. Don't pour them out to drain—you want them to be dripping a bit with water. Turn on the heat under the saucepan to medium. Twirl the noodles around in your sauce. Then add half the cheese and twirl again. Once the cheese is mixed in, add the rest. You might need a couple of spoons of the pasta water if it gets dry.

4. Serve at once. If you want to get fancy, you can sprinkle a tad of nutmeg on top and call it mountain dust.

This recipe makes enough for four people. Or for one yeti.

Bigfoots are believed to have a special fondness for peanut butter and bacon, which is why this Bigfoot-Long Sandwich might just be the ultimate squatch lunch.

Bigfoot-Long Sandwich

One twelve-inch baguette

Six to eight pieces of bacon

Peanut butter

* Optional: honey or pickles (but not both—Bigfoot is an omnivore but not crazy)

1. Cook the bacon in a skillet set over medium-high heat, turning it every so often so it gets uniformly crispy. You might need a grown-up's help with this.

2. Put a piece of paper towel on a big plate and drain the bacon there once it's cooked.

3. Slice your baguette in half.

4. Cover both sides generously with peanut butter.

5. If you're using honey or pickles, put them on top.

6. Add the bacon, close your sandwich, and enjoy!

This is enough sandwich for two to four people. Or one bigfoot.

Butternut Squatch Soup

One butternut squash

One onion

Four cups of chicken broth

Two tablespoons of butter or olive oil

Salt and pepper to taste

1. Preheat your oven to 400 degrees.
2. Ask an adult to slice the squash in half (squash are really hard and cutting them is kind of a chore).
3. Put the squash on a cookie sheet, cut side up, and roast it about 45 minutes until the insides are soft.
4. Take it out of the oven and let it cool.
5. As it cools, dice one onion into small cubes. Put two tablespoons of butter or olive oil into a soup pot and cook the onion in it over medium heat until the cubes get soft and clear. You don't want to use such high heat that they turn brown.
6. Scoop out the soft, roasted butternut squash. Put it into the pot with the cooked onion. Gently stir in the chicken broth. Bring it to a boil, and then simmer for about 15 minutes, stirring as you go. Season it with salt and pepper until it tastes good. Serve!

This makes enough soup for four people. Or one sasquatch.

Abominable Snowcones

One box of cake mix—any flavor you like.

Two dozen flat-bottomed ice cream cones

Two dozen cupcake liners

One tub of vanilla frosting

1. Preheat your oven to 350 degrees.
2. Make the cake batter according to the recipe on the box.
3. After lining each indentation with a cupcake liner, pour the batter into a muffin tin until each reservoir is two-thirds full. Put an ice cream cone upside down over each one—the cake will rise into the spot.
4. Bake for 16 to 22 minutes.
5. Let your snowcakes cool. Don't be in a rush or your frosting will get melty.
6. Peel off the papers. Frost and then top with a sprinkling of sugar so it looks like sparkling snow.

This makes enough cupcakes for a party of twenty-four or so. Or one yeti.

SPOTTED!
"One of the Scariest Things Ever"

Kristy Aho and her husband, Dale, were hunting grouse in the woods of Minnesota. Their prey took off and Dale got off his four-wheeler and followed it. As soon as he walked in the woods, he passed a sasquatch.

"That's when it jumped and ran away," he said.

Kristy swears it's true. "I seen it, the whole side of it come through this little clearing, every time it took a step, the two of us were just shaking, my heart almost stopped."

The creature was seven and a half or eight feet tall and covered in long, dark-brown hair that you could see through all the way to its skin. "I knew what it was right away," Kristy said, "but I, I didn't wanna believe it, and it was one of the scariest things ever."

Chapter Five
FAMOUS BIGFOOT HUNTERS

THE *FINDING BIGFOOT* FOUR

Cliff Barackman

Cliff Barackman has loved both music and science since he was a boy growing up in Long Beach, California. Now, talk of bigfoot sightings is music to his ears—and it has been since he was in college, when he first realized the animal might be more than just a legend.

He read lots of books in his college library and came to believe bigfoot is biologically possible. He brought that knowledge with him to the great outdoors and on his first bigfoot expedition—to the famous Bluff Creek area in 1994—he found possible bigfoot tracks, damaged trees, and hair that looked squatchy. He's been hooked ever since.

Cliff is especially interested in footprint casts and has one of the biggest collections of them in the country. They're a great form of physical evidence in support of sasquatch, and Cliff is a big believer in gathering and analyzing data (he's the best at math in the bunch). He also used to be a teacher and is great at explaining complicated things about bigfoot in ways everyone can understand.

He's still interested in music, by the way—he studied jazz guitar in college and sometimes plays gigs around his adopted hometown of Portland, Oregon.

Matt Moneymaker

Matt is the founder and president of the Bigfoot Field Researchers Organization (BFRO). He's a lifelong bigfoot fan, starting when he was just an eleven-year-old kid watching a number of documentaries in the 1970s. As a college student at the University of California–Los Angeles, he started talking with bigfoot researchers in the United States and Canada.

And then, in 1987, his life changed forever. He found his first track in the mountains of Ventura County, California. After that, life took him from the West Coast to the Midwest in the early 1990s, but he never left his interest in bigfoot behind. He learned about the many bigfoot sightings Ohio farmers had made in the previous decade, and then had his own first encounter in 1994, as he camped overnight in a swampy wildlife refuge south of Kent, Ohio.

In 1996, just as regular people started using the Internet regularly for the first time, Matt founded the BFRO, which helped connect researchers around the Web site and blog. The BFRO publishes and investigates reports of sightings by eyewitnesses, and they have a Web site you can visit and explore for all sorts of information about the creatures, as well as sightings that have been made.

In 2000, he organized the BFRO's first big expedition, to a place called Skookum Meadows in Washington State, where a team found what is believed to be a bigfoot body print. He coproduced television programming about bigfoot and also organized trips where researchers would seek out the creature all around the country. He still does this today, in addition to his work on *Finding Bigfoot*.

Matt has popularized many new techniques in sasquatch hunting:

- He helped promote the use of sound blasting and howling to find bigfoot and the first to record "the Ohio howl," a long, moaning noise believed to have been made by a large, male sasquatch.

- He was the first to connect piles of dead deer with bigfoot, after Mennonite farmers in Ohio pointed out the strange stashes to him.

- He was the first to formally present a paper on knocking sounds made by bigfoots at a 1992 International Society of Cryptozoology conference at Rutgers University.

- He organized the first public expeditions to gather observations and evidence in various parts of North America.

- His organization was the first to debunk the "Georgia Bigfoot Body" hoax in the summer of 2008.

Ranae Holland

She's come a long way since her girlhood in Sioux Falls, South Dakota. Now she's a research biologist and field biologist who regularly works for the National Oceanic and Atmospheric Administration.

But even when she was a kid, Ranae Holland was interested in bigfoot. It was during the 1970s that she and her dad used to cozy up and watch bigfoot movies and documentaries together, so sasquatch has a special place in her heart even if she can't quite wrap her brain around believing the creature exists.

That's right. Ranae Holland *doesn't* believe in bigfoot. But that doesn't stop her from tromping through the woods with the team in search of evidence.

Her role is to help the guys think critically and ask themselves what other explanations could account for the sightings that people have reported. It's sometimes a tough spot to be in, being the only skeptic surrounded by some of the most passionate squatchers in the world.

But Ranae loves helping people think critically by considering evidence, asking questions about it, and coming up with credible explanations. She also loves being in the outdoors. Camping, hiking, fishing, and kayaking are some of her favorite activities. Mix in bigfoot and real science, and she's as happy as could be.

James "Bobo" Fay

James "Bobo" Fay grew up surfing sasquatch-size waves in Manhattan Beach, California. By the time he was in college, though, he'd left the beach behind for the woods of northern California, where he hoped to find bigfoot.

After college, he worked as a logger on Native American crews with the same goal in mind. He hoped to learn enough about their legends that he'd finally experience some sightings out in the wild. That day came in 2001, when he was on an investigation with John Freitas, a veteran bigfoot researcher. The experience rocked his world.

Bobo is a big guy. He's six feet, four inches tall, which makes him a great stand-in for bigfoot when the team is reenacting sightings. This important research technique lets witnesses re-create what they saw, helping understand the creature's size and behavior. This can help the team validate or rule out a sighting.

Bobo is also accomplished at making bigfoot calls.

Today, when he's not with the *Finding Bigfoot* crew, he works as a commercial fisherman out of Eureka, California. He also does odd jobs that can bring him closer to bigfoot.

BIG NAMES IN BIGFOOT HISTORY

Over the years, many people have devoted their lives to finding bigfoot. Here are some of the most notable:

Tom Slick

Tom Slick was a man with an aptronym—a last name that suited him. Born to a wealthy family that made its money in the oil business, he was a bit like a character out of a movie: a brash Texan who founded an airline, hung out with the eccentric billionaire Howard Hughes, advocated for world peace, and funded scientific research institutions he hoped would revolutionize the stodgy science frontier.

He thought the yeti was the missing link between humans and apes (even though anthropologists and biologists are already well aware of many species linking humans to earlier primate forms).

In 1957, Slick traveled to the Himalayas' Arun Valley in search of the yeti, interviewing people who said they'd had encounters. They found track and samples of yeti scat, and the experience whetted their appetites for a bigger hunt that would be covered by the *New York Journal-American*, something Slick thought of as "the Ultimate Quest." He was confident enough they'd snag a yeti that he bet a friend $1,000 he'd have one in hand within a month (although he didn't go on the second mission himself—he had people for those things). He lost the bet, but his team estimated there were four thousand small yetis living in the Himalayas. In all, he spent $100,000 on three yeti hunts, expecting the abominable snowman would someday soon be found.

Slick also funded the Pacific Northwest Expedition to find bigfoot. It started in 1959, again with high hopes. But the searchers didn't trust each other or get along well, and the discovery didn't happen during his lifetime. On Sunday, October 6, 1962, his private plane crashed near Dell, Montana. Slick and his pilot died.

SPOTTED!

Seeking Wisdom from the First Nations

In their search for sasquatch, the *Finding Bigfoot* team is willing to try anything, including a traditional cleansing ceremony with members of the Stoney-Nakoda tribe in the Canadian Rockies.

Lenny Wesley, a tribe member, explained how they would burn ten different types of medicinal plants in a sacred smoke ceremony meant to help the foursome cleanse themselves and tap into the power of sasquatch.

"What you see is not just hiking trails," Lenny said. "There's more beyond those mountains. There's power."

It's a sort of a sixth sense that lets the bigfoot researchers tap into the creature's power and follow it wherever it might lead, a technique they recognized as unusual, but one worth respecting as they walked the Stoney-Nakoda land.

John Green

This newspaperman originally thought stories about a sasquatch were hooey, and when a Swiss man named René Dahinden stopped by Green's newspaper office to inquire about sightings in 1956, he told the man as much.

It's understandable. Green was the son of a Canadian cabinet minister and a lumber heiress. He grew up in cities. But, knowing newspaper readers always enjoy interesting stories, he put a bit in the paper about Dahinden's interest in a North American yeti. That's when people he respected talked about the Ruby Creek incident from 1941, where a giant, hairy creature broke into a woman's storage lean-to and scared her out of her wits.

He put his journalistic mind to work, interviewing the son of the sheriff's deputy who had investigated the sighting. The deputy, who had since passed away, had been thorough. He'd made sketches and casts of the footprints. A lawyer and former magistrate had also interviewed witnesses and taken sworn affidavits (signed documents used as evidence in court). You can be convicted of a crime called perjury if you lie in one, so this was evidence Green took seriously, concluding there was maybe something to this sasquatch thing after all.

In 1958, when Jerry Crew reported the Willow Creek footprints, Green and his wife visited. June Green found one as soon as she stepped out of their car.

John Green told an interviewer at a University of British Columbia alumni magazine, "What particularly impressed me was the similarity between the outline of these tracks and the tracings I had of one of the Ruby Creek footprints."

Later, he was instrumental in the famous

Patterson-Gimlin film, which is said to show a female bigfoot walking beside a creek. Green brought Roger Patterson to the Bluff Creek area of northern California where the film was shot. Patterson said he captured his famous footage a month later.

After the movie touched off a bigfoot craze, Green—always methodical—started a database of sightings. He recorded four thousand of them, stopping when his database technology grew out of date. He wrote many books about the lengthy search and estimated he sold 250,000 of them. His most famous is probably one he wrote in 1978, called *Sasquatch: The Apes Among Us*. He did all this while raising four children, being a competitive sailor, and holding local political office. He also founded the World Sand Sculpture Contest, which paved the way for record-setting sculptures in sand. (Look them up online—they're really incredible.)

He was never discouraged by the media reports that Ray Wallace had faked those 1958 tracks that made so many people believe in Bigfoot, even if the news widely reported that Bigfoot "died" with Ray Wallace in 2002.

"The fact is that the tracks exist, and no human being has yet proven to be able to replicate the tracks of the depth recorded. I'd like to know what's making the bloody tracks," Green told the alumni magazine.

BIGFOOT WITNESS PHOTO

Bob Titmus

By trade, Bob Titmus was a taxidermist, someone who specializes in stuffing dead animals and making them appear lifelike. But the real work of his life was the search for bigfoot. In 1958, after Jerry Crew found Bigfoot tracks in the Bluff Creek area, Titmus taught Crew how to make plaster casts of footprints. Not long after that, Titmus and a friend found slightly smaller sasquatch tracks that made people think more than one creature was afoot.

He also was the first leader of the Pacific Northwest Expedition to find bigfoot, which was funded by the millionaire Tom Slick. After he moved to British Columbia, Titmus collected a ton of tracks (plus knee- and handprints). Finally, he cast the tracks at the site of the Patterson-Gimlin encounter.

Many believe footprints are the best evidence for bigfoot we have.

SPOTTED!
There Is No "P" in Bigfoot

Keith Hamilton is an experienced outdoorsman. He hunts, fishes, camps, hikes—if you can do it in the woods, he's a pro.

But one night as he was settling into sleep inside his tent in a patch of wilderness a forty-minute hike from the trailhead, he heard something unusual . . . heavy footsteps.

"I heard it slowly coming closer and closer to me," he said.

And then the truly strange happened. He heard a sound, a stream of liquid hitting his tent. It was raining steadily outside, but this particular noise sounded different. So he opened the flap of his tent five or six inches to investigate.

That's when he saw it.

"A figure that was about twice the width of my shoulders," he said. "The hair on my neck just stood up, because this is not normal."

And what was the creature doing?

Peeing. A lot.

Keith describes it as a "strong, steady stream." His theory is that the bigfoot was urinating on his tent to mark it.

He had time to see the creature's full upper torso, shoulders, and head. Based on a re-creation, the *Finding Bigfoot* team estimates it to be an eight-foot-tall male.

No word on how Keith cleaned his tent, but after his sighting, he was hooked on sasquatch hunting.

René Dahinden

Intrigued by tales of the Himalayan yeti, René Dahinden heard about sasquatch when he was working on a farm in Alberta, Canada. Finding the North American version became his life's work. He worked alongside John Green do to this, and hunted bigfoot for fifty years, even choosing the pursuit over his wife and family. He also cowrote a book called *Sasquatch/Bigfoot: The Search for North America's Incredible Creature* in 1973.

Over the years, he collected hundreds of footprint casts that he took with him on his travels. He also interviewed legions of people who claimed to have encountered bigfoot and had choice words for skeptics who didn't think footprints mattered.

"If anyone finds this kind of evidence immaterial," he said, while holding a heavy plaster casting, "let me strike his head with it."

The pipe-smoking Dahinden wasn't a fan of university-educated scientists.

"Those clodhoppers!" he once told a magazine reporter. "Science is the pursuit of the unknown. Now maybe the scientists think there is nothing unknown, since they know it all, and therefore they don't have to pursue it. I don't know, it looks like the scientists get up every morning and pray, 'Please God, let me go through another day without a new thought.' "

He was equally scornful of people who faked evidence and encounters.

Dahinden bought the rights to show the Patterson-Gimlin film, and he created a sensation in Moscow when he showed it to a roomful of scientists, but he never made much money showing it, and he supported himself by gathering the lead out of spent shotgun shells at a gun range, gathering hundreds of pounds of it using his bare hands.

Before he died, he admitted some disappointment and possibly even doubt with his lifelong quest. "You know, I've spent over forty years—and I didn't find it. I guess that's got to say something."

Look closely. Can you see bigfoot?

Peter Byrne

When he was a child in Ireland, Peter Byrne's father used to tell him bedtime stories about the yeti. As a young man, Byrne spent years in the Himalayas, and later—once he was convinced by bigfoot tracks and Native American lore—he traveled across five continents in search of bigfoot. He led three major trips in the Pacific Northwest.

He later helped launch the Bigfoot Information Center in The Dalles, Oregon, during the 1970s, and the Bigfoot Research Project in the Hood River in the 1990s. The second project, which lasted five years, seemed to have a better chance for success because of its prime location near the Cascade Mountains. They used better technology, including remote sensors. They had a hotline for sightings and a helicopter.

They didn't find a bigfoot, but they did find several sets of huge footprints, along with eyewitness reports. They also found a giant, nine-foot-by-four-foot bed of moss, "which one of the creatures almost certainly constructed and in which it slept," he reported.

All these years later, he's still continuing what he calls The Great Search. His goal at this point is to extract DNA because "scientists will accept absolutely nothing less as evidence."

Ivan Sanderson

Ivan Sanderson was a Scottish explorer who became an American citizen and one of bigfoot's biggest boosters, even though he wasn't always taken seriously. His big idea was to turn the study of bigfoot into a science called ABSMery. He didn't like the term abominable snowman, so he took letters from it and married it to a suffix that gave the study a bit more respectability.

He was a follower of an early twentieth-century writer named Charles Fort, who collected articles and other tidbits about things that science couldn't explain, and in 1965, he started the Society for the Investigation of the Unexplained, which published its own *Pursuit Magazine*. In addition to many articles, he wrote *Abominable Snowmen: Legend Come to Life*, which was published in 1961.

When Sir Edmund Hillary dismissed the yeti as mere legend, Sanderson was one of the many who objected. Later, Tom Slick paid him to hire John Green, René Dahinden, and other serious bigfoot seekers.

In addition to bigfoot, Sanderson was also interested in UFOs and wrote a book called *Invisible Residents: The Reality of Underwater UFOs*, which speculated, among other things, whether long-ago alien visitors had built themselves underwater docking bases. For some people, this sort of interest and theory discredits his interest in sasquatch.

Roger Patterson and Bob Gimlin

This duo is famous for shooting the first film footage of a bigfoot. In October 1967, they took a break from making a movie about the creature in Washington State, and traveled down to Humboldt County, California, to check out a new set of tracks that had been reported. The rain washed them away before the men arrived, but on a horseback ride one afternoon in the Bluff Creek area, they rounded a bend and spotted something astounding: a furry creature with a human-like head, long arms, and obvious female body parts. They filmed the creature, and the resulting clip has been held up as both a hoax and the holy grail of the bigfoot search.

Patterson, who died of cancer in 1972, was a bit of a scoundrel who had hoped to make a lot of money from the movie, which did not help his credibility. But Gimlin never made any grand attempt to capitalize on the incident, nor was he characterized as anything less than an honest man.

Paul Freeman

One of the most controversial figures in bigfoot history was a man named Paul Freeman, who in 1982 was going about his job as a United States forest ranger when he found bigfoot tracks near Walla Walla, Washington. He also had a sighting and straightaway contacted a biologist and the state's border patrol. Ultimately, there was no official government report about it.

Depending on whom you talk to, Freeman was either a truly gifted bigfoot seeker—he found many footprints—or a persistent hoaxer. Anthropologists like Grover Krantz and Jeff Meldrum were on Freeman's side. They found the dermal ridges on the tracks to be persuasive, and Meldrum even bought Freeman's track collection in order to study it. Other people, especially Dahinden, thought Freeman found too many tracks to be credible.

Whatever the case, before his death in 2003, he found many footprints, handprints, and even a bigfoot buttock-print. He also captured what he claimed was video of bigfoot, which you can search for online.

Daniel Perez

This devoted bigfoot scholar is author of *Bigfoot at Bluff Creek,* the definitive account of the Patterson-Gimlin film; *Bigfoot Notes*, a bibliography of the many things that have been written about the creature; and editor and publisher of the *Bigfoot Times,* a monthly newsletter that is considered essential reading for bigfooters.

Perez also founded the Center for Bigfoot Studies and has one of the biggest collections of books and bigfoot files anywhere.

Wolf Henner Fahrenbach

This Berlin-born scientist earned his doctorate in zoology from the University of Washington and a postdoctoral fellowship in anatomy at Harvard Medical School. He also ran the electron microscope lab at the Oregon Regional Primate center for thirty years and has expertise in everything ranging from insect morphology to cell biology.

In short, he's a scientist with fantastic credentials—but unlike the scientific mainstream, he's a firm believer that the Patterson-Gimlin film is genuine.

Fahrenbach has written many scientific articles about sasquatch and its body size, and is an expert in identifying suspected sasquatch hair. As recently as 1999, he identified a dozen hair samples he believes belong to the creature.

THE ABSMery AND INTERNATIONAL SOCIETY OF CRYPTOZOOLOGY

Over the years, people fascinated by hidden animals—cryptids or cryptozoids—have tried to be organized in their approach to finding animals such as bigfoot and the Loch Ness Monster, a massive, dinosaur-like creature believed to inhabit one of Scotland's largest, deepest freshwater lakes. Their goal was to turn the study of these animals into a proper science.

Ivan Sanderson kicked off the first of these, naming it the ABSMery. Supporters didn't end up finding bigfoot or making much of a scientific contribution, but it did give the creature more attention. Sanderson wrote many articles about wild men and published them in a magazine called *Fantastic Universe*, which was printed from 1953 to 1960. (He didn't only write about wild men. One of his articles was titled "What Pilots a UFO?")

Later came the International Society of Cryptozoology, which was set up in 1982 in

Washington, D.C. Unlike the ABSMery, the ISOC focused on gathering and evaluating evidence for all "unverified animals." By this, they meant ones that had been encountered or had left tracks or other evidence, but had not yet been recorded by scientists. They also included creatures that were no longer thought to be living but actually were, a category that would include something like the Loch Ness Monster.

Bernard Heuvelmans, who coined the term cryptozoology, was the group's president. The organization used an image of an okapi on its logo, honoring an animal that looks like it was built from parts of a zebra and a giraffe and had been thought to be a local central African legend until 1901, when a British explorer sent a pelt home to London. From 1982 to 1996, the ISOC published a journal called *Cryptozoology*. Alas, the group ran out of funding in 1998.

BIGFOOT FIELD RESEARCHERS ORGANIZATION

While the International Society of Cryptozoology was headed toward extinction, the Bigfoot Field Researchers Organization was just taking off. The organization, started by Matt Moneymaker, is focused exclusively on bigfoot-type creatures, and its members approach the topic scientifically by collecting physical evidence from suspected bigfoot habitats and doing their best to understand what the evidence can reveal. They also aim to do no harm to bigfoot, so, unlike certain hunters, would not kill a bigfoot to prove the creature exists.

Unlike earlier groups, the BFRO was born in a time of sophisticated technology. A centerpiece is their database of bigfoot sightings. It's a great place to figure out where you should start your own search for bigfoot (see Chapter 6 for more information on that). You can search for sightings by region, and you can also look for the most recent reports. If you're into even more technology, you can install Google Earth and zoom in on sightings, viewing the actual topography from above.

You can also join the BFRO yourself, but it's not easy. The first thing you have to do is join one of their four-day expeditions, which are scheduled around the United States and Canada. There is a $300 to $500 fee, and you have to be over twenty-one or traveling with someone at least that old. You also have to be an experienced camper (although you can in some cases get a motel room). After you've successfully completed one of their expeditions, a member has to recommend you.

If this sounds like too much, you can report sightings to their database. Be warned that they don't look kindly on hoaxers. But if you did go camping and saw tracks, gathered other evidence such as hair, or encountered a bigfoot, you can visit the site to report what you saw or found, when you saw it, where you were, and whether there was anyone else with you. They'll also ask you for your contact information in case one of their volunteer researchers needs to get in touch with you for more information.

SPOTTED!
Things That Go Thud in the Night

Sisters Lonni Olson and Donna Ross are new to the pursuit of bigfoots. A series of strange incidents that happened when they were camping in the woods left them rattled.

It started at three o'clock in the morning; after a long night of searching, Donna had lain down in her tent. Something went thud outside.

"I sat up immediately and I took a look around," she said.

The next morning, when she investigated by daylight, she found a rock nearby. But that wasn't all.

Lonni said there were indentations in the ground. "Not footprints, per se, but the grass had absolutely been stepped on."

The next night, around nine thirty or ten o'clock, just as the sun was setting, they heard a tree knock and some growls, a deep, guttural sound that affects you like no other.

"It's hard to explain," Lonni said, "because it kind of goes through your body."

The experience has them convinced that sasquatch turned the tables on them—turning the hunters into the hunted.

PRO TECHNIQUES

Want to search for Bigfoot like a professional? You might try using one of the *Finding Bigfoot* team's techniques. Some require special equipment, but many are relatively simple.

Vocalizing and knocking:

Bigfooters believe the creatures communicate with each other by whistling, making loud whooping and shrieking noises, and by knocking rocks against trees. You can do the same to see if you get a response. To practice your bigfoot call, you might go to BigfootSounds.com and listen to the samples.

Projecting audio:

If you have a portable music player with speakers, you can blast sounds that might be interesting to a curious Sasquatch. The *Finding Bigfoot* team has projected the sounds of a crying baby, for example.

Glow sticks and bait:

The *Finding Bigfoot* team once suspended a bunny in a cage from a tree. Then they hung glow sticks that would move if anything disturbed the cage. (Don't worry—the bunny was fine.) Instead of using live bait, you might try putting food in the cage and seeing if a bigfoot goes for it.

A Ghillie suit:

This is a sort of hair- and leaf-covered camouflage suit used by some hunters and snipers to disguise themselves in the woods. It was originally invented by Scottish hunters, but was then used for military reasons in World War I. The *Finding Bigfoot* team has used a Pied Piper kind of technique with a Ghillie suit, making themselves visible with lights as they try to lure a sasquatch into traveling alongside them in the woods. You would want to be very careful with this method. Instead of using it as camouflage, which can be dangerous, combine it with lights and noise to call attention to yourself.

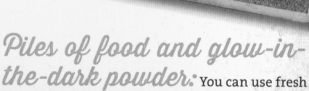

Piles of food and glow-in-the-dark powder:

You can use fresh fruit, peanut butter, Zagnut bars, bacon, raw liver, or other favorite bigfoot treats for this. Just set out a pile of food somewhere squatchy, sprinkle glow-in-the-dark powder on top, and follow the footprints wherever they lead you. (You can buy this powder at science supply stores.)

MORE ADVANCED TECHNIQUES AND EQUIPMENT

The Dark Man Technique is recommended for grown-ups only. To use it, one person sits alone in the woods with no lights or electronics whatsoever. The goal is that a sasquatch will pass by.

Use a drone camera if, say, your family just won the lottery. These expensive, lightweight flying contraptions can be guided by remote control. The *Finding Bigfoot* team used one during the first season of the show.

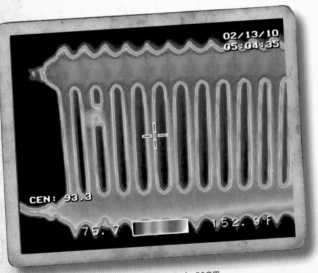

This radiator is HOT.

Thermal imagers detect anything that gives off heat, turning it white on the screen. You can tell if whatever you've picked up is wearing clothing (bigfoot travels in the buff), and you can also gauge its size. If you spot a nine-foot creature on your thermal imager, you're on to something. If you want to get super-fancy, you might borrow a vehicle built by the FLIR Corporation, which comes equipped with a thermal camera that can pick up anything from a hundred meters to nine miles away.

"I've literally dreamed about things like this a thousand times," Bobo Fay said when the *Finding Bigfoot* team took a spin in one.

What about a blimp?

One team of bigfoot researchers tried to raise $355,000 to build the ultimate stealth sasquatch tracking and recording device. The Falcon Project would have sent a blimp up to patrol forests at night with a high-definition thermal camera, silently sending back images from remote areas likely to be home to bigfoot. They unfortunately fell short of their fund-raising goal by a maddening $343,135.

SCIENTISTS FOR SASQUATCH

Your average scientist will probably be squeamish about sasquatch. It's not because he or she is afraid of coming across one but, rather, because no one has for absolute certain encountered one despite a lot of looking. Logically speaking, the longer it takes anyone to find a bigfoot, a body, or a set of bones, the less likely it is that such a creature exists to be found. To some scientists, it seems silly to continue looking.

Scientists are also kind of clubby. They follow one another's work, share information, compete, and collaborate to push the frontiers of what is known and understood. If you're a scientist who believes something different from the mainstream, it can harm your reputation in the same way eating something really different for lunch at school might (say, freshly cooked tarantula seasoned with salt, sugar, and a whiff of garlic, which is apparently delicious, like soft-shelled crab).

Not every scientist has been scared off of the pursuit of bigfoot, though. When a body print called the Skookum Cast was found, the renowned chimpanzee expert Jane Goodall said it was worth studying. She surprised a lot of people when she told a National Public Radio inter-

Jane Goodall, chimp expert.

viewer she was certain large undiscovered primates like yeti and sasquatch exist.

"I've talked to so many Native Americans who've all described the same sounds—two who have seen them," she said in the September 27, 2002 interview.

She later seemed to backpedal just a bit in a *National Geographic* interview, where she said, "I'm fascinated and would actually love them to exist."

Some scientists, however, have done even more than hope for bigfoot.

Grover Krantz

Back in the 1960s, when people got a little wild and when the University of California at Berkeley was a wilder spot than most, one student stood out for being perhaps the wildest of them all. His name was Grover Krantz and he became a campus legend for holding parties that lasted all night—and all the next day.

In addition to the parties, he was also known

for having smart conversations and unusual ideas. One of his hobbies growing up was collecting the skeletons of animals. In college, he wrote a paper about the small differences between coyote and dog bones. Despite all the partying, he did graduate and got a master's degree at Berkeley, but an argument with a professor stopped him short of getting his doctorate. He later finished that at the University of Minnesota, with a PhD dissertation titled "The Origin of Man."

It must have been fun watching Krantz work. For one experiment, he wore a fake eyebrow ridge for six months so he could figure out what the structure did for *Homo erectus,* an extinct species of upright-walking hominid that lived from 1.8 million to 300,000 years ago, spreading from Africa to Spain, Georgia, India, China, and Java.

He became a professor at Washington State University, where he taught and studied evolution, with a special focus on skeletons. He published books and articles that focused on the anatomy of bigfoots based on tracks, making observations about things that separated bigfoot prints and tracks from human ones.

For example, he did not believe there was any evidence bigfoot had opposable thumbs, which would mean they also lack something called a thenar pad. On your hand, that's the fleshy part at the base of your thumb.

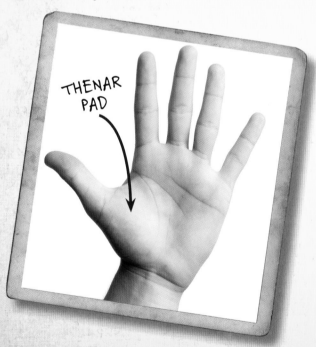

THENAR PAD

He also thought sasquatch feet and human feet were differently proportioned. Sasquatch toes are all one length. Their feet are flat with a long heel and relatively short forefoot. And the balls of their feet appear in some prints to be split in two. He was the first scientist to establish this with tracks, his fans say. He also noted skin ridges, sort of like fingerprints, on some tracks. Called "dermatoglyphs," these were different from the prints of humans and other animals.

He definitely got people's attention. With certain tracks, other researchers agreed there was something notable. A set of tracks in the snow called the Cripplefoot tracks had been made by a creature that could spread its toes, according to a professor at the University of Groningen. And a fingerprint expert at Scotland Yard said the prints were "probably real." Krantz also gave his expert opinion on the authenticity of important bigfoot evidence, such as the Patterson-Gimlin film and the Skookum body print.

Krantz was protective of his research. According to the book *Bigfoot: The Life and Times of a Legend* by Joshua Blu Buhs, Krantz wrote notes in code and had a couple of secret methods he believed allowed him to separate authentic footprints from the hoaxes, although apparently one determined hoaxer in 1996 made a fake that fooled him by pouring mud into a box of cat litter, shaping a print, and marking it to look like it had toenails and scars. After Krantz said it was the real thing, the construction worker revealed his fakery. Instead of admitting he was fooled, Krantz tried to argue that the construction worker was only pretending it was fake so he could later embarrass Krantz by saying it was real—not a very likely scenario.

Krantz believed that bigfoot was a surviving Gigantopithecus and even proposed a scientific name for the creature, *Gigantopithecus blacki*, although that was rejected because there was no actual body to study. (He didn't give up, trying again with another name and a research paper published on naming a creature using footprint evidence. Both were rejected.)

After Krantz died from pancreatic cancer on Valentine's Day in 2002, he began his last lessons for students. He donated his body to the University of Tennessee's "body farm." Scientists there study how quickly bodies decompose, which is useful for people investigating suspicious deaths (you can work backward to figure out when a person might have died based on the state of the body).

Then, in 2003, his bones were sent to the Smithsonian—the same place he sent the bones of his giant dog, a beloved Irish wolfhound named Clyde. They're on display there together.

Carleton Coon

Carleton Coon was an anthropologist who taught at Ivy League universities. Although he specialized in prehistoric farming communities as well as contemporary tribal societies, he had a keen interest in wild men and he had some ideas about what they might be—intelligent primates living in secret in remote lands.

In an essay called "Why There Has to Be a Sasquatch," he wrote:

It is easier to say what they are not than what they are. They are not Neanderthals. Neanderthals had beaky noses and brains bigger than those of most men alive today. They had fire and flaked sophisticated tools. They were not dropped out of flying saucers. It is unlikely that they are the unaltered descendants of our ancestors. They are fellow primates. They are smarter than we are in the sense that they can live without modern inventions, in apparently every climate, even deserts, if the latter are within walking distance of mountains and water. It is less costly and easier to find out what they are than it is to dig up our fossil ancestors, and possibly theirs, in lands now torn by war and seething with newfound national pride. If we don't destroy the atmosphere, it may be they who have the better chance to survive, if it is true that the meek shall inherit the earth.

John Napier

John Napier was the director of the Primate Biology Program at the Smithsonian Institution in Washington, D.C. He wrote a book called *Bigfoot, The Yeti and Sasquatch in Myth and Reality*, and was one of the rare mainstream scientists who took the time to consider evidence of bigfoot. He believed it was reasonable to devote a small amount of the money spent on scientific research toward unsolvable, outrageous, and offbeat topics.

This didn't make him a believer by any stretch, but he was at least willing to investigate, and he weighed in on some of the biggest bigfoot findings of the twentieth century.

He was one of the people who helped debunk the Minnesota Iceman of 1969 (see Chapter 9), and described how, early on, he was legitimately excited to see this find.

"In those early days this seemed a very exciting prospect," he said. "I drafted a rather pompous press release indicating that although the Institution was somewhat skeptical, it was open-minded enough to cooperate fully in the investigation."

He also reviewed the Patterson-Gimlin film, which he thought was probably a hoax. But he believed that indirect evidence of bigfoot, especially footprints, held enough interest that sasquatch couldn't be dismissed outright.

Roderick Sprague

Roderick Sprague was an anthropologist at the University of Idaho and editor of *Northwest Anthropological Research Notes*, the rare scholarly journal that let people submit articles about sasquatch. With Grover Krantz, he also edited *The Scientist Looks at Sasquatch*, a two-volume collection of articles written by scientists about various aspects of bigfoot research, including how you can calculate their weight from a footprint.

Jeffrey Meldrum

Jeffrey Meldrum is the academic heir to Gordon Krantz. A professor of anatomy and anthropology at Idaho State University, he's a tireless and creative researcher who believes that the evidence gathered to date about bigfoot demands scientists to keep pursuing the truth—even if it's unpopular.

He was eleven years old when he first saw the Patterson-Gimlin film, a subject he covered thoughtfully in his book, *Sasquatch: Legend Meets Science*. He also has a huge collection of footprint casts (more than two hundred), some of which look like hoaxes, but others that show all sorts of things that convince him they're real: musculature, skin impressions, and even "pressure ridges" caused by sasquatch's flexible foot bending in the middle.

Although his fellow scientists aren't jumping on the bigfoot bandwagon, they respect his expertise and dedication.

"He does bring more scientific rigor to this question than anyone else in the past, and he does do state-of-the-art footprint analysis," David R. Begun, a paleoanthropologist at the University of Toronto, told *Scientific American* magazine in 2007.

Meldrum also edits *The Relict Hominoid Inquiry*, a free online journal that publishes papers about possible relict hominoids—ancient forms of humans believed still to be alive and undiscovered. The papers are peer reviewed, which means other scientists have looked at them and determined they are responsible scholarship. (You can read it online here: www.isu.edu/rhi)

John Bindernagel

Since 1963, John Bindernagel, a PhD scientist, has been searching for bigfoot. In 1998, he wrote *North America's Great Ape: The Sasquatch*. He has collected tracks and heard alleged sasquatch sounds that reminded him of a chimpanzee's whoop.

Chapter Six
READY, SET, SQUATCH!

PREPARING FOR YOUR OWN
BIGFOOT EXPEDITION

So you've decided to set out and find bigfoot for yourself. This puts you in excellent company. Smart, adventurous people from around the world have been seeking proof of bigfoot for ages, turning up all sorts of tantalizing and fascinating clues in the woods, in swamps, and atop the world's highest mountains. Over the years they've cataloged footprints, hair samples, and handprints. They've stolen bones, studied curiously mangled deer, and pored over audio recordings of mysterious shrieking animals.

What hasn't been found, though, is definitive proof: a bigfoot skeleton or a living specimen.

But that doesn't mean *you* won't be the one to make history. The famous French biologist Baron Georges Cuvier was completely wrong in 1852 when he said, "There is little hope of discovering new species" of large animals. At that time, Westerners thought gorillas were mythical creatures. We know today these species are as real as peanut butter sandwiches, a food bigfoot would probably like, given the creature's apparent fondness for peanut butter. (Various bigfoot researchers have left peanut butter products and entire jars of the spread as bait, according to Matt

Moneymaker. One bigfoot seeker even left out a Zagnut bar and it disappeared at the same time a thermal camera recorded a sasquatch-shaped figure swiping the treat from a stump, much to the excitement of bigfoot fans. Could Zagnut be a sasquatch's favorite candy bar? Maybe!)

At any rate, new species are discovered all the time—maybe even someday by you.

If you are going to find a bigfoot, you have to be smart about it. You have to know what to bring, where to look, and how to gather your evidence. Also? Getting a parent's approval is essential. But don't worry. We've got you covered.

WHERE to LOOK

In each place there have been bigfoot sightings, the elusive creature is called something different: sasquatch, yeti, skunk ape, yowie. No matter what the giant primate is called, though, there have been sightings around the world.

Your best bet for spotting your own sasquatch might be someplace close to home. For sure, your parents are more likely to go for that as your next family trip instead of, say, Indonesia or Nepal. It's a good idea for a first-time bigfooter to be practical and get some experience before heading off to the world's most remote and exotic places.

Here's a chart of bigfoot hotspots in the United States. Which one is closest to your home?

STATE	SIGHTINGS	MOST RECENT	LAST POSTED
Washington	554	Feb-13	Nov-12
California	426	Aug-12	Oct-10
Florida	236	Feb-13	Dec-12
Oregon	232	Nov-12	Aug-12
Ohio	230	Feb-13	Aug-11
Illinois	210	Feb-13	Dec-12
Texas	193	Sep-12	Nov-11
Michigan	164	Feb-13	Nov-12
Colorado	113	Feb-13	May-12
Georgia	109	Feb-13	May-12
Missouri	102	Dec-12	Sep-12
New York	101	Jul-11	Sep-10
Pennsylvania	100	Oct-12	Mar-12
Kentucky	90	Jan-13	Nov-12
Oklahoma	86	Nov-12	Apr-12
Tennessee	85	Jan-12	Oct-11
West Virginia	85	Jan-13	Nov-12
Arkansas	82	Jan-13	Sep-12
North Carolina	79	Mar-12	Jan-12
Indiana	73	Jul-12	Jul-11
Arizona	71	Feb-13	Oct-12
Idaho	67	Jul-11	Nov-09
Utah	67	May-12	Dec-08
Alabama	65	Jun-12	Apr-11
Wisconsin	64	Feb-13	Sep-13

STATE	SIGHTINGS	MOST RECENT	LAST POSTED
Iowa	61	Jan-13	Oct-12
Minnesota	55	Oct-12	Aug-11
Virginia	53	Jan-13	Oct-12
South Carolina	51	Nov-11	Feb-12
New Jersey	46	Aug-10	Jul-10
Louisiana	40	Apr-11	Feb-10
New Mexico	40	Oct-11	Jan-12
Montana	38	Feb-13	Nov-12
Kansas	36	Feb-13	Jun-12
Maryland	32	Dec-12	May-11
Wyoming	28	May-10	Mar-10
Alaska	23	Aug-10	Jan-13
Mississippi	21	Sep-12	Oct-10
Massachusetts	19	Apr-12	Mar-12
South Dakota	17	Aug-11	Jun-08
Nebraska	14	Jun-11	Aug-08
Maine	13	Mar-04	Feb-04
New Hampshire	10	Nov-09	Jun-09
Connecticut	8	Jul-09	May-09
Nevada	8	Apr-09	Feb-05
North Dakota	6	Dec-10	Aug-05
Vermont	6	Jan-06	Oct-05
Rhode Island	5	Dec-11	Nov-11
Delaware	3	Dec-12	Jan-04

TOTAL SIGHTINGS: 4317

GETTING PERMISSION

If you tell your parents, "I'm going to find bigfoot. Smell ya later!" they're likely to grab you by the straps of your backpack and pull you back indoors. This is not because parents exist to stomp your dreams into tiny bits. No, one of their jobs is to keep you safe. Your parents can actually be your best bigfoot-hunting allies. Here's how to get them on your side.

Tell your parents you're interested in studying primate evolution. Almost any word that comes after "studying" is going to fill your parents with glee. But "primate evolution"? That's irresistible. (And in case they ask, *primates* are large mammals, including apes, chimps, and humans. *Evolution* describes the way generations of living things change and grow more complex over time.)

Explain that they don't even need to believe in bigfoot to be fans of the creature. This way, if your parents are skeptics, you can give them a way to rationalize the trip to their curious friends, relatives, and neighbors.

WHAT NOT TO SAY

Bigfoot is mostly nocturnal so we'll have to stay up all night. Break it to them gently later, like when you're already en route to the woods. Tell them to think about all the stars they'll get to see.

Sasquatches are super-strong and can throw heavy objects long distances. Definitely don't quote Bobo Fay, who says, "It's a known fact sasquatches throw rocks. Any sasquatch researcher will agree to that and [sasquatches]'ll do it to protect their feeding areas. We've got over a thousand reports in the BFRO database of rocks being thrown in conjunction with bigfoot activity." Although the *Finding Bigfoot* team and other experts have heard accounts of tire-size logs and basketball-size rocks being launched at people, there aren't a lot of reports of people being injured this way, so you can keep this tidbit to yourself. Likewise, there is no need to mention that bigfoots like brushing up against tents, behavior often reported by people who claim to have encountered bigfoots,

Remind them that hands-on learning is the most effective. Something like this is called "field study." Again, there's that *study* word!

It will be a fun, affordable trip for the whole family. Even if you'd rather go by yourself, forget it. If you're going to be serious about your sasquatch search, you're going to have to cover a lot of ground and this means you need an adult to drive you. But they don't need to worry that this will be a budget buster, because you'll be sleeping in a tent instead of a hotel. Bigfoot doesn't hang out at the Holiday Inn—not even at the complimentary waffle bar.

including members of the *Finding Bigfoot* team. Information like this will just scare your poor parents.

Sasquatches are more likely to approach women, who are smaller and therefore less threatening, according to members of the *Finding Bigfoot* team, which in the past has had their resident skeptic, Ranae Holland, raise a ruckus in the hopes a sasquatch would show its face (it didn't work, but then again, Ranae is six feet tall and in great physical shape). Anything that suggests your mom is the most likely to have an encounter will flip her wig, and not in a good way. Didn't we already tell you not to freak out your parents?

Bigfoot poop can be huge. According to the BFRO, a potential sample spotted in Florida's Rock Springs State Park contained segments that were up to eleven inches long. Yes, it is a fascinating thing to note. But it's the sort that tends to cancel out all the positive effects of the word *study*.

PACKING YOUR GEAR

Expert hikers recommend a list of ten things you should have with you when you venture into the wilderness. Even if you aren't planning to be out overnight, you should always have this gear with you in the woods because you never know what might happen. Here's what you need for any outdoor adventure, in addition to sturdy shoes and weather-appropriate clothes:

☐ 1. navigation device
    (map and compass or GPS)

☐ 2. sun protection (sunglasses
    and sunscreen)

☐ 3. extra clothes

☐ 4. a headlamp
    and/or flashlight

☐ 5. first-aid supplies
    (also bug repellant
    and bear spray)

☐ 6. stuff to make fire (waterproof
    matches/lighter/candles)

☐ 7. tools—a Swiss Army knife,
    duct tape, a whistle,
    walkie-talkies

☐ 8. extra food

☐ 9. extra water

☐ 10. a tent or tarp

There's also special gear you'll need just for your bigfoot expedition.

At the top of the list? **A camera.** Few of the thousands of bigfoot sightings in the United States were made by people equipped with one. If you don't own one, see if you can borrow one. Your school might even have one you can check out with permission from a science teacher or librarian.

Not only can you use the camera—still and video are good—to capture photographic evidence of a bigfoot, you can also record the terrain for review, just in case you missed something the first time around. What's more, some of the most famous images and videos were shot accidentally. The people who captured them didn't know what they had until they

reviewed their footage and photographs later. Photographs a man named Randee Chase took at Silver Star Mountain in Washington State are some of the best suspected bigfoot pictures, and they were pretty much shot by accident.

Many bigfooters prefer video cameras because they can record the creature's howls, moans, rock taps, and other sounds they're known to make. If you capture footage, experts can also use it to stage reenactments and better understand the nature of what you caught on your video.

What else belongs in your bigfoot expedition kit? All sorts of things you can use to gather evidence, including samples of hair, footprints, and even poop.

Dental Stone, Hydrocal, or similar material to take casts of footprints. Plaster of Paris works too, but the experts like Dental Stone better because it's harder.

A bowl. This is to mix the plaster and water in.

A magnifying glass. This you can use to examine small things, such as hair samples.

Tweezers. Use these to pick up the hair.

Plastic bags in several sizes. Use these to store hair and other evidence.

Latex gloves. More than one pair, please. Remember . . . you might be gathering poop, known to researchers as "scat."

A tape measure. Use this to measure the length of tracks you find, the distance between them, and the height of twisted-off branches that might be signs of passing bigfoots.

Binoculars. If you see a possible bigfoot in the distance, these will come in handy.

A field journal. Any notebook you can hold in your hand will do. It's probably best to have one that you use just for bigfoot expeditions, so it doesn't get cluttered with other things. You can use the notebook to record all sorts of observations: what you saw, what you heard, and what you smelled (Bigfoot is said to stink to high heaven. For more on bigfoot body odor and what might cause it, check out Chapter 8). It's also important to write down *when* you had these observations. Take notes about other animals you observed and even things you didn't see that you expected to, just to have a well-rounded record.

A "scale item." When you take a picture of a bigfoot track, put something next to it for scale. The mountain climber Eric Shipton used his ax. You could use a can of soda or something else that can be measured and gives a later viewer a quick idea of the track's size. (But don't forget to take measurements and make a cast.)

Why study SCAT?

Poop is gross, but it's also a treasure trove of information that reveals what a creature eats and whether it's in good health. Bigfoots are omnivores, which means they eat meat and plants. You might find seeds, plant parts, or even hair and bones in its droppings. Likewise, if you find the droppings of animals bigfoots are believed to eat (such as deer), then you know a food supply exists that makes it possible for the area to support a sasquatch.

Some extra-fancy things you can bring if you're an extra-fancy person

Illuminated pushpins. If you're tracking bigfoot at night, you can mark your route with thumbtacks that light up.

A parabolic listening device. This is spy gear—it's a shallow bowl, sort of like a miniature TV satellite dish with a microphone attached. (You can make one yourself. A couple of Web sites tell you how. Use the keywords "parabolic listening device instructions.")

A GPS device. You can use it to mark your route and record the exact location of evidence you gather and see.

Night-vision goggles. Think of how handy these would be on Halloween, too.

11:33 PM
Matt & Cliff

This is what peering through night-vision goggles looks like.

±3.8 °C
A
30.8
-30.6

The Finding Bigfoot crew . . . in thermal vision!

Professional equipment serious sasquatch hunters use

Thermal cameras: These are sensitive to body heat given off by living creatures. Experts look at the shape of the readings and determine the animal it most likely belongs to.

Trail cameras: These can detect motion and photograph passing animals.

Drone planes: These unmanned flying devices are equipped with cameras and can travel to areas too remote for humans.

SPOTTED!
Bigfoot: A Cereal Killer?

Bobby Greffrath was driving in the Catskills when he saw something lying in the road: a grocery bag, and from the looks of it, there was a box of cereal inside. He swerved to avoid it . . . and then something darted behind his car.

He glanced in his rearview mirror and saw a massive, hairy thing.

"So I keep driving," he said, "and as I turned the corner there's something—an over-seven-foot-tall creature walking on two feet right on the side of the road."

The creature stepped behind a tree and darted into some tall grass. Bobby was dumbfounded and acutely aware that he was the only human around.

"I didn't know what to make of it," he said. "I've never seen something like that walk on two feet before. I was alone, and I just didn't know what to do."

The *Finding Bigfoot* team's verdict: a squatch sighting.

WHAT TO LOOK FOR:
TELLTALE SASQUATCH SIGNS

While it would be great fun to stroll through the woods and happen upon a bigfoot napping in a glade of ferns, that's not exactly likely to happen. Think of yourself as a detective hunting for clues big and small.

FOOTPRINTS: They call the creature bigfoot for a reason. The best footprints can be found in muddy areas, so keep your eyes peeled. A study of more than seven hundred prints by Dr. W. Henner Fahrenbach, PhD, showed the average length is just over fifteen inches. Footprints are very important clues, too. Researchers can tell all sorts of things about animals by the prints they leave behind, not only how big they are, but also whether they walk upright—and sometimes even what they eat.

NESTS: These aren't just for the birds. Large primates such as gorillas make nests, and bigfoot is believed to do the same. Look for sticks and branches that have been twisted off and arranged into clumps. Some believe bigfoots dig holes and conceal them with branches, as well. The nests are said to be smelly.

HAIR SAMPLES: Bigfoot sheds, and these hairs are some of the best evidence a field researcher can gather, because scientists who study genetics can test them. Sometimes, this is disappointing. In 2005, for example, hair samples gathered in Canada turned out to have come from a bison. But other samples haven't been matched to any known animal. Intriguing! Bobo Fay says utility poles are a great place to look for evidence because animals use them as scratching posts.

SCAT: Not only are bigfoot droppings super-size, they can potentially be full of all sorts of interesting things, including plants, hair, eggs, and larvae. Although there are no scat samples tied to Bigfoot with 100 percent certainty, sasquatch hunters leave no stone unturned when it comes to the pursuit. Many have gathered samples of suspicious droppings, which are said to have an "eye-watering" odor, according to an article by a biologist in *Beautiful British Columbia Magazine*.

The BFRO says the droppings can be up to four inches wide and three feet long, and they're shaped like sausages. Witnesses have watched bigfoot do its business, wipe itself, and then lick its hand. So yes, the whole scat business is disgusting. But this is science. It's not for wimps.

BROKEN BRANCHES: Sasquatches are said to twist branches off, perhaps as trail markers. If you see twisted-off branches, particularly big ones out of reach of human hands, you might have just found a bigfoot path.

EYE SHINE: At night, bigfoot's eyes are said to reflect light. Look for the shine to be much brighter than human eyes.

Why do some animals' eyes GLOW at night?

Some animals have a special reflective surface behind their retinas. This extra inner-eye mirror helps them see better at night. And it's kind of a backup plan. When light hits the eye, it's supposed to hit something called a photoreceptor. But if it misses, this reflective surface—called a *tapetum lucidum*—acts like a mirror. It bounces the light back to the photoreceptor for one more try.

Many animals have tapetum lucida: cats and dogs, deer, cattle, and horses. Humans, apes, squirrels, pigs, kangaroos, and many other primates *don't* have them—even though bigfoot is said to, according to many eyewitness accounts, including members of the *Finding Bigfoot* team. If a bigfoot or sasquatch is found, no doubt the presence of a tapetum lucidum in a hominid would be of great interest to scientists.

HOW TO MAKE A CAST

Your best bet at finding a good footprint is to look near soft, damp soil. Just as you do, Bigfoot gets thirsty, so if you can find a river or creek, it's worth looking closely for prints.

When you find one you like, clean it up a bit. Remove any twigs, leaves, or pebbles, but be careful not to mess up the print. Even if you're not sure it's good enough to preserve, err on the side of caution.

"When in doubt, cast it," Cliff Barackman says.

Mix your Hydrocal with water, following the instructions on the package. You'll want to mix slowly so you don't get a lot of bubbles in it. Let it sit a moment until the bubbles stop rising. Then tap the side of the bowl gently, just to make sure you've gotten rid of all of them.

Once your mixture is smooth, pour it gently into the print. Now comes the hard part: waiting. It will take at least thirty minutes, and even then, your print will be very fragile, so wait longer if you can stand it. While you're waiting, you can write field notes or look for more prints nearby, making sure to measure the distance between them if you find a second or third.

Are there power lines nearby?

Don't forget to look for power lines. Sasquatches are often seen around them, Cliff Barackman notes—and with good reason. "Power lines represent one of the few places that sunlight reaches the forest floor, and therefore gives us rise to highly nutritious plants that deer and other herbivores need to survive."

The Sasquatches, in turn, hunt the deer and other herbivores.

WRITING GOOD FIELD NOTES: A GUIDE

There's no such thing as "sloppy copy" in field notes. You're not supposed to rewrite them more legibly at some date in the distant future, when your hand has stopped cramping or when it's stopped raining. Field notes are supposed to be the very document you wrote when you were making your observations. Some field notes have become really famous, like the ones Charles Darwin took on his voyage to the Galapagos Islands. If you spot a bigfoot, your notes will be *invaluable*, which means they will be worth so much money no one can put a price tag on them.

Also, take your time to make your handwriting legible, or you might be very sad when you look at your notes a few weeks later and can't figure out what you were writing about. One expert tip: Write your notes *before* you collect your sample. That way, you aren't trying to juggle your notepad and a giant sack of bigfoot evidence.

FIVE THINGS TO INCLUDE IN EVERY ENTRY

Number each sample separately. Write the number in the notebook and on your plastic bag. Sharpie works best for this, but it will stain your clothes, so be careful and put the cap on tightly.

Describe the sample. What does it look like? What does it smell like? How big is it?

Identify where you found it. The more accurate you can be, the better. This is where a GPS device can be very handy.

Describe your surroundings. Are you by a river? Surrounded by trees? On a mountain slope? What kinds of plants are growing nearby? You can shoot a photo or video to accompany your description.

You should also note the date, time, location (with GPS coordinates if you have them), the weather, and the names of the people you're with.

Sample #17: Three possible sasquatch hairs. All medium brown, approximately three inches long, one of which is covered in mud or possible scat. Found on a telephone pole in Bluff Creek area of Humboldt Forest. Telephone pole was next to a stand of mixed vegetation, including Redwoods and ferns.

Date: April 28, 2013

Time found: 3:47 p.m.

Witnesses: Corey, Sean, and Rick

GPS Coordinates: 32.8400° N, 117.2769° W

SPOTTED!
An "In Tents" Experience

Robert Boyd and his girlfriend had found the perfect campsite off a trail in New York's gently sloping, thickly wooded Catskill Mountains. He'd just pitched his tent when the footsteps began: distinctive, heavy thuds that stopped just out of the range of his vision.

He ducked inside the tent and something started throwing objects, first on one side of the tent, then on another. It got scarier from there.

"Next thing I know, the tent is being pushed in," he said. The pushing motion was down and sideways, a common pattern, according to Cliff Barackman.

What's more, Robert said, someone—or something—on two legs was doing it. There's "no, no way" it was a four-legged creature, or quadruped.

The footsteps "were loud. They sounded heavy. They sounded very deliberate . . . definitely bipedal." And they were louder than Cliff's reenactments.

Even though Robert didn't see a sasquatch that night as he was huddled in his tent, all signs point to the presence of one, Cliff said. "Most of the time, people don't see them."

IF YOU SEE BIGFOOT

Stay calm! As Bobo Fay puts it, "Don't point at it, you don't run at it . . . just . . . film it."

As you record your sighting with your camera, take care not to make a lot of noise that would spook the sasquatch. If it sees you back, don't look straight at its eyes, because this is the sort of thing that animals perceive as a challenge. Just stay calm and quiet, and move slowly. You might even sit down and pretend to eat a snack or pick fleas out of your pelt. Don't even think about running. The bigfoot is probably extremely fast and has a longer stride than you, which means it can cover more ground more quickly.

Afterward, once you are in a safe location, fill out your field guide with everything you can remember, and then report the sighting to the Bigfoot Field Researchers Organization.

WHEN YOU GET HOME

If you got really lucky and saw a bigfoot or found evidence, hurrah! If you didn't make a sighting, don't feel bad. Even bigfoot researchers who have been at this for decades don't always hit the jackpot. But what separates you from almost everyone else in the world is that you tried. If you have evidence such as hair samples or footprint casts, you can share these with your fellow bigfooters. Save all your research. And as soon as you feel ready for more adventure, you can try again.

Persistence is everything. "There's no more important trait to a bigfooter than perseverance," Cliff Barackman says, "because skill comes with perseverance."

THREE
SASQUATCH SIGHTINGS

"This is getting creepy"

Troy, North Carolina, is a small town with a big legend: that its streets are paved with gold. It's kind of true—the fill dirt used beneath the pavement came from a gold mine, and a few sharp-eyed sorts have found nuggets. Since 1978, though, another kind of hunt has become even more thrilling.

Everything changed for this little hamlet on the edge of the Uwharrie National Forest in 1978, when Bigfoot sightings began in a flurry. Soon, locals were obsessed with the creature that seemed to be secretly living alongside them, sparking all sorts of speculation and gossip. "What could it be?" people wondered.

Kevin Green doesn't wonder what the mystery creature is. He's convinced it's a sasquatch—and one that guards its turf jealously.

The night Kevin saw a bigfoot, he and his buddies were camping. They'd just lit a crackling fire and were making their dinner when the first of a volley of rocks was launched from the woods.

"We tried to ignore it," he said. This proved impossible. "The rocks were just pelting, like flying through the air, at us."

They were like baseballs, he said, and all through the night, the rocks kept coming. His friend Brad was sleeping when one struck the tent's wall. It was unsettling, to say the least.

"I remember he said, 'One just hit my tent. This is getting creepy. I want to go home.'"

It got scarier from there as they heard a low growl coming from the direction of the rocks. Now, Kevin is left with the unforgettable impression he'd been trespassing in bigfoot's habitat, upsetting the creature. "They were just like mad at us for getting in their way," he said.

"They see these eyes, and they have a different glow"

Central Oregon is a place of spectacular beauty: farmland, former logging towns, mossy woods, and rolling mountains. It's also the heart of Bigfoot country in the Pacific Northwest. Since 1950, Oregon has been home to almost 1,300 bigfoot sightings, many of which are concentrated within the Willamette Valley. The Willamette National Forest consists of more than one and a half million acres of pristine woodlands, run through with 1,500 miles of rivers, lakes, and streams that can support a great deal of wildlife.

Rusty Carroll and Brady Berglund were fishing in central Oregon's Molalla River when someone hurled a rock at them. Then the screaming started.

"We hear two . . . screams coming in from the opposite direction," Rusty said.

Their pal Nolan, who was fishing with them that evening, held up a light and slowly scanned the banks of the river.

"Hey, guys," he said. "Look at this."

The trio saw a pair of glowing, amber-colored eyes glide slowly behind a tree on the opposite riverbank. The mysterious eyes were the most amazing hue.

"I've never really seen anything that color," Brady said. "It's tough to explain." What's more, the eyes were large, round, and spaced far apart. "It looked like it was floating almost, the way those eyes moved through the woods."

They took pictures. When they went back the next day to take a cast of the footprint, they found another and measured the animal's stride with a piece of fishing line: a whopping fifty-three inches. Given the smooth gait of the creature they saw, this could only have been made by an animal with extremely long legs (a shorter creature taking such big steps would have lurched up and down more). The friends felt sure they'd seen a bigfoot.

But they weren't quite right. It wasn't *one* sasquatch they encountered that night on the riverbank, the *Finding Bigfoot* team believes. It was two—the screams they heard were from the other, calling out to its hairy companion in the darkness.

A giant at the edge of the cemetery

Ryan Harris's family lives near a cemetery in Washington State. He patrols the edge of his family's land quite a bit, looking for animals as well as vandals and thieves. That's what he was doing one night when he noticed something on the right-hand side of the road. It didn't look quite right, so he stopped his car and flicked on the high-beam headlights.

"I watched just for a few seconds and it seemed to move a little bit," he said. "And the next thing I know, it takes a step into the road— one step halfway across the road, next step it was off in the brush on the left-hand side of the road."

This creature that could cross a road in two strides was bipedal. It had grayish-brown, matted fur. It was probably seven feet tall. And in all Ryan's years of patrols, he'd never seen anything like it.

"I've seen every animal there is to see in these woods," he said. "I've seen bear. I've seen cougar. Nothing has ever given me the feeling that this gave me."

It made the hairs on the back of his neck stand up. His body shook. His heart raced. He was afraid—overwhelmingly so.

"As soon as I got my composure back I, I went through in my head many times, *What did I just see?*" he said. "I know that it stood on two legs, and was larger than myself, and walked across the road in two steps."

Could it be a prankster in a sasquatch suit? He doubts it. Why would an extraordinarily large human dress up at nine thirty or ten o'clock at night and goof around on the edge of Ryan's property? And there was no way a human could cross a road that wide in just two steps, he said. (When Bobo reenacted it on behalf of the *Finding Bigfoot* team, it took him three, and he was really trying.)

"There's not in my mind any way that a human could possibly do that," Ryan said. "It was definitely not, in my mind, a human."

Chapter Seven
BIGFOOT SPOTTED

BIGGEST HOTSPOTS IN NORTH AMERICA

People used to keep track of all the bigfoot sightings by hand. Now, though, we can use computers and databases to get a better idea of where a bigfoot is most likely to be found. The best of these is the one kept by the Bigfoot Field Research Organization, which keeps records of sightings in the United States and Canada. If you see one, you can go online and report it using their form. A volunteer might even contact you for more information.

The database has more than 4,300 sightings in the United States, and nearly 300 in Canada. Some states and provinces report more sightings than others.

THE TOP TEN STATES FOR BIGFOOT

Where are you most likely to see bigfoot? Based on a percentage of overall sightings, these ten states have had more sightings than any others.

Washington: almost 13 percent of bigfoot sightings occur here
California: almost 10 percent of bigfoot sightings occur here
Florida: about 5.5 percent of bigfoot sightings occur here
Oregon: about 5.4 percent of bigfoot sightings occur here
Ohio: about 5.3 percent of bigfoot sightings occur here
Illinois: about 5 percent of bigfoot sightings occur here
Texas: about 4.5 percent of bigfoot sightings occur here
Michigan: about 4 percent of bigfoot sightings occur here
Colorado: about 2.6 percent of bigfoot sightings occur here
Georgia: about 2.6 percent of bigfoot sightings occur here

The numbers change a little when you factor in how populated the state is. For example, Oregon, which has fewer residents than Florida and Ohio, has more bigfoot sightings per capita, so it moves up the list. Here's how many sightings these top ten states have had per 100,000 residents. The higher the ratio of sightings to population, the more likely *you* are to have your own. (We rounded these numbers just a bit to keep them manageable.)

Washington: 8 per 100,000 residents

Oregon: 6 per 100,000 residents

Wyoming: 5 per 100,000 residents

West Virginia: 4.5 per 100,000 residents

Idaho: 4.2 per 100,000 residents

Montana: 3.8 per 100,000 residents

Alaska: 3.2 per 100,000 residents

Arkansas: 2.8 per 100,000 residents

Utah: 2.4 per 100,000 residents

Oklahoma: 2.2 per 100,000 residents

THE FIVE **WORST** AREAS FOR BIGFOOT SIGHTINGS

If you *don't* want to see a bigfoot, you might travel to Vermont, Rhode Island, or Delaware. Sightings are so rare in those states that they represent less than one-tenth of a percentage of the total reports. In fact, Delaware might have to update its official state slogan from "We're first!" to "We're third-to-last . . . in bigfoot sightings!"

You are even less likely to see bigfoot in Washington, D.C.—which makes sense because a sasquatch wouldn't be caught dead in a suit and tie. There have been zero sightings in the nation's capital. Likewise, no bigfoots have been seen in Hawaii. It actually might seem worrisome if they have, because how would a bigfoot have traveled from the mainland to the islands, which have never been connected to the continental United States or Asia by a land bridge?

In CANADA

If you want to see a sasquatch up north, the best place to be is in British Columbia—just north of the Washington State border. Quebec, on the other hand, is *not* the place to see a sasquatch. Here's how it breaks down by province:

British Columbia: about 44 percent of sasquatch sightings
Ontario: about 24 percent of sightings
Alberta: about 13 percent of sightings
Manitoba: about 11 percent of sightings

From there, sasquatch sightings **REALLY** drop off:

New Brunswick: about 2 percent
Saskatchewan: about 2 percent
Yukon: less than 2 percent
Quebec: less than 2 percent

Certain provinces and territories—Newfoundland and Labrador, Prince Edward Island, Nova Scotia, Nunavut, and the Northwest Territories—reported no sightings at all.

TYPES OF SIGHTINGS

There are three types of bigfoot sightings in the Bigfoot Field Researchers Organization database: Class A, Class B, and Class C.

But these aren't like school grades. A sighting doesn't get an A for being interesting, or if the person who saw it seems like he or she is definitely telling the truth. Rather, it has to do with how certain we can be that the sighting was of bigfoot and not something else.

Class A: This is the most certain type of sighting. If a witness got a clear look at a bigfoot and can rule out any other animal, or if there are well-documented footprints that can't be attributed to any other animal, then squatch hunters consider this a Class A sighting.

It doesn't have to be in person. The Jacobs Photographs (see Chapter 2), taken by trail camera, show a creature with limbs too long to be a baby bear. Bigfooters have ruled that animal and others out, so the sighting gets the top rating.

Class B: Let's say you were far away, or you had your bigfoot encounter at night. Or let's say you didn't see a bigfoot, but heard vocalizations. This kind of sighting is a Class B, because there's a potential for misidentification.

Experts don't look at Class B reports as less valuable or credible, and sometimes they can be so detailed they're quite compelling. For example, a former police officer took a hunting trip to Mud Spring on South Dubakella Mountain in Trinity County, California, in 1998. He described squatchy sounds in great detail on the BFRO Web site. You might include this level of detail if you ever make a report to the organization:

The whole area was extremely quiet, even in late afternoon/dusk when many animals begin to venture out. I saw only two ravens and a couple blue jays, the entire time I was there. No squirrels, no deer, and no noise.

As many of you know, the forest has solitude but is far from silent.

I had made a small fire that evening. I do not normally make a fire when backpacking, but because I had a fire ring available, a plentiful supply of deadwood, and it had been years since my last trip, I decided to enjoy one.

I turned in at about 2150 hours [9:50 PM], and was asleep within minutes.

At about 2230 hours [10:30 PM] . . . I was awakened by the sound of a large snapping branch. It was not a branch falling, and the branch gave a cracking noise that made it sound like it was a thick branch. Even though my eyes snapped open with the sound, I just lay in my sleeping bag listening. I didn't move.

Then with my head close to the ground resting on my ground pad, I heard it. Not the clop of

hooves or the padding of paws, but the dull, vibrating thud of footsteps! I nearly defecated in my sleeping bag. I was keenly aware of what I was hearing, and I could feel the adrenaline in my veins.

The footsteps were to the northeast of my tent, when first detected. My hearing was trained in that direction because that is the same direction I heard the branch snap, too. I estimated them to be ten to twenty feet away, judging from the vibration and sound. Two more steps and the thing making them was in front of my tent, about five to ten feet away. Then the footsteps faded to the southwest with two more footsteps.

I was lying there scared to death, thinking about what I was going to do, when all of a sudden, my pots down at the kitchen moved and clanged together! I was not imagining anything now, and knew it was not a dream! I grabbed my headlamp and illuminated my tent, trying to drive off my visitor.

After I waited about two minutes, I looked out my tent and saw nothing. I pulled on my boots and walked to my kitchen area. There I found my nested cookware pots un-nested, and spread out. What ever un-nested those pots had thumbs!

Class C: The final category is for second- and third-hand reports. So if someone told you a story about their sighting, or if it was a "friend of a friend" kind of tale, or even a story with sources that can't be traced, this would count as a Class C report. The BFRO does keep them in their archives but only rarely makes them public unless they happened before 1958, the year the "Bigfoot" name was attached to sightings in the media.

SPOTTED!
Bigfoot Versus the Biker

In 1974, Bud Garcia was out riding his ten-speed bicycle in Rhode Island when he noticed one of his brakes had come loose. He stopped to fix it—and that's when he heard a series of loud footsteps.

"That's where I see it step out," he said, "this white gorilla. And it chased me right down the road."

But before the creature caught him, it pivoted and leapt over a wall and into a thatch of brush and tall grass. Bud spied on the six-foot creature, noting its pointed head, broad shoulders, big arms, and barrel chest.

He thought it was a gorilla, but Matt Moneymaker thinks otherwise. In southern Ohio during the 1980s, there were numerous sightings of a white bigfoot. Likewise in the mountains behind Big Sur, California. And it's probably an old one, he says. After all, elderly bigfoots get gray hair—just like we do.

BIGFOOT TRAP

Why don't people just build a bigfoot trap and catch one already? People have, and what is believed to be the world's first and only bigfoot trap still stands in southern Oregon.

An organization called the North American Wildlife Research Team built the trap in 1974, near a spot where a miner had spied what appeared to be bigfoot tracks in his garden. The trap stands in a fairly remote site in the Rogue River National Forest, near the Oregon-California border, though it can be reached by the Collings Mountain hiking trail.

As traps go, this one's huge—over eight feet tall and roughly ten feet square. Its sides are wood, and on one end a gate of green steel slides down to contain an unlucky sasquatch.

For years, the North American Wildlife Research team baited and monitored the trap. But all they ever caught were bears. Now the trap no longer works and is mostly an item of curiosity for tourists.

GPS INFO FOR THE TRAIL AND TRAP #943 TRAILHEAD GPS
N 42°03.073' W 123° 07.903'

BIGFOOT TRAP GPS
42.056567, -123.137233

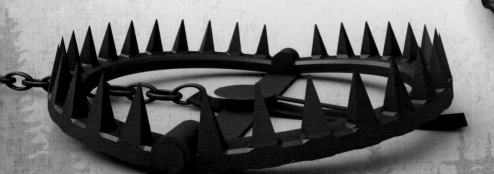

Chapter Eight
THE SCIENCE OF SASQUATCH

It is not uncommon for them to come in the night and give three whistles. Then the stones will begin to hit the houses. The people are troubled with their nocturnal visits.

—A letter from Rev. Elkanah Walker to the American
Board of Commissioners for Foreign Missions, 1840

When it comes to established animals, it's possible to know all sorts of interesting facts about them. For example, an African elephant can be up to eleven feet tall, weigh between 7,000 and 13,200 pounds, and live sixty to seventy years in dense forests and on open plains. They also eat plants and try to avoid humans, their top predator.

When it comes to cryptids, we have to take our best guesses about their behaviors, habitats, diets, and life spans. These aren't blind guesses, though. We use evidence we find, other observations we make, and facts about similar animals to build a reasonable picture.

Here's the best thinking about where bigfoot might live, what the creature might eat, and how it might behave.

Habitat

Although bigfoot sightings have occurred in most states and in many Canadian provinces, most sightings tend to be in remote, forested regions with plenty of sources of protein. They also require sources of water.

Bigfoot is believed to make use of certain human technology, though—power lines in particular. They're not powering their nests, though. They're traveling.

As Matt Moneymaker puts it, "Power lines are significant because sasquatches travel along power line routes. They can walk along them at night. They know they're not gonna run into any people. It's really kind of their highway."

But it's not just that. Where power lines have been built, trees have been removed. This changes the environment in a way that helps bigfoots, Cliff Barackman says. "Power lines represent one of the few places that sunlight reaches the forest floor and therefore gives us rise to highly nutritious plants that deer and other herbivores need to survive. And as it turns out, Sasquatches are hunting the deer and other herbivores."

Diet

Bigfoots are omnivores, which means they eat plants and animals. (See How They Hunt, What They Eat, p. 111.)

Social organization

Unlike gorillas, chimpanzees, and bonobos, which live in groups, a sasquatch is a more solitary creature—possibly like orangutans, which are occasionally seen in groups of two or three when there's enough food to go around. Some bigfooters do believe the creatures live in small family groups. (One famous bigfoot encounter even involved a man named Albert Ostman, who claimed he was kidnapped by a family of bigfoots—a mom, a dad, and two kids.) Bigfooters also believe these nocturnal animals communicate with each other by shrieking, whistling, and knocking tree trunks.

Sasquatches wouldn't be seen in groups like these—they're believed to be more solitary creatures.

SPOTTED!
Father-Son Sasquatch Sighting?

Chris Patterson and his father, Jeff, had followed a trail through a dense, deciduous forest tall enough to block out much of the sun's light. As they stood in the semidarkness, they heard a noise. Jeff switched on his camera.

There, on the embankment just ahead of them, stood a large dark creature.

"It almost seemed like it was looking right directly at me," Jeff said. "And then it reached out and grabbed a tree and he just started pulling on the tree."

They could hear the roots crack, and instinct took over. They were too close to this creature, whatever it was. Jeff reached out, grabbed Chris by the arm, and the two took off.

"This creature was tearing down this tree," Chris said. "I thought we better get out of there in a hurry."

The two feel there's no chance it was a hoaxer in a costume, which fit like real skin. "It was form fitting," Jeff said.

When the *Finding Bigfoot* four visited later, they found the lower half of the tree the animal had torn at. Bobo was able to reenact the tree shaking, which means Chris and his dad couldn't rule out the possibility that it was a human, but the location itself felt like a prime habitat—good enough for the team to investigate further.

BEHAVIOR AROUND HUMANS:
ARE THEY DANGEROUS?

Of all the thousands of sasquatch sightings over the years, there have been hardly any reports of attacks on humans. It's not uncommon for a bigfoot to chuck rocks at people, to make scary sounds, or to brush its hand along tents.

But actual attacks are almost unheard of. There was the incident in Teddy Roosevelt's book where a human was killed. There's an old Native American tale, echoed in a similar early-twentieth-century account, that claims a bigfoot abducted a woman, who later gave birth to a half-bigfoot baby that died shortly afterward.

But in modern times, no sasquatch has been accused of harming a human. Eyewitnesses say the animals retreat when they are spotted—especially when someone shines a bright light.

While they aren't harmful to humans, this isn't the case for animals, though. Wildlife such as deer, elk, raccoons, beavers, ducks, and rodents are on the bigfoot menu. The same goes for livestock. Sasquatches are believed to swipe chickens, rabbits, and pigs when given the chance. And, according to the Bigfoot Field Researchers Organization, aggressive dogs have been found dead and surrounded by bigfoot tracks.

BIGFOOT BY THE NUMBERS:

SIZE: The average height is seven feet, ten inches, according to measurements from eyewitness reports and projections based on footprint length. The biggest bigfoots are believed to be taller than ten feet.

WEIGHT: The average weight is about six hundred fifty pounds, but they might grow to be over a thousand pounds, based on some of the largest footprints.

FOOT LENGTH: Of more than seven hundred footprints collected over a fifty-year period, the average length is fifteen and a half inches. Tiny bigfoot prints as small as four inches have been seen, all the way up to twenty-seven-inch whoppers. The "median" length is sixteen inches. How is this different from the average? It means half of the footprints are longer and half are shorter.

The *Finding Bigfoot* team measuring possible bigfoot strides.

SKIN COLOR: Varied, from black to charcoal to browns and red-browns. It's lighter on their palms and soles.

HAIR COLOR: Generally dark, including black, brown, and reddish. But gray-white hair has been spotted on older bigfoots. Can range from matted to glossy and clean. Females are reportedly cleaner. Hair can range from three inches to two feet long.

"Sasquatches basically look like a combination of human and ape," Cliff Barackman says. But because of their long lives and their low reproductive rate, there are going to be a lot of differences between two different bigfoots, he says—just as there are between two different people.

WHAT DO BIGFOOT BABIES LOOK LIKE?

According to reports gathered by the BFRO, bigfoot babies are something only a mother could love. One eyewitness claims to have seen a small and "ugly" bigfoot baby. Baby bigfoots are believed to be born weighing about four pounds after a gestation period of about nine months.

Young sasquatches are typically born between the months of February and May, grow rapidly, and stay with their mothers until they are about ten years old and six feet tall.

Sometimes, young offspring are found in remote areas with lots of food nearby. "Native Americans have told me on several occasions that sasquatches drop off their juveniles in certain areas I call nurseries," Cliff says. "These nurseries have some things in common, such as an abundance of food and plenty of places to hide."

A BIGFOOT'S BODY: WHAT IT'S LIKE

No one knows for sure what bigfoot's skeleton might look like, but the late bigfoot scholar Grover Krantz thought it might be a relict giant ape named *Gigantopithecus blacki*, the humongous ape that lived in southern China (see Chapter 3 for more on this creature).

Krantz reconstructed a skull based on the partial jawbone that is among the only fossil evidence of this mammoth ape. It shows a big-eyed creature with a ridge of bone running from the front to the back of the skull, otherwise known as a sagittal crest. The creature's mouth and squarish, human-like teeth protrude (but less than an ape's), and its spine runs straight down from the skull, as with other bipedal animals.

Eyewitnesses have told the BFRO the creature has a heavy brow ridge, prominent cheekbones, and a square jaw. Bigfoots also have a flat nose, thin lips, and human-like ears that are usually covered by hair.

Is Bigfoot HAIRY everywhere?

According to the Bigfoot Field Researchers Organization's data, Sasquatches have hair just about everywhere, but the lengths vary. It's long on the head and ears, but short on the face (although some male Bigfoots sport mustaches and beards). Their forearm hair is long. Both males and females have hairy chests, and their private parts are similarly obscured. Their lower legs are like hairy bell-bottoms, and they have hairy butts.

"Bigfoots in general are covered in hair from head to toe, except for maybe the palms of their hands and the soles of their feet, and the tips of their noses," Matt Moneymaker says.

Continuing down the body, bigfoots have powerful neck and back muscles, which is why one might turn its body along with its head to glance over its shoulder (the Patterson-Gimlin film's most famous frame depicts this). Its shoulders are wider than human ones—about 40 percent of its body height, as opposed to 25 to 30 percent that you tend to see in people. Bigfoots don't have great posture. They lean forward about fifteen degrees.

They have big, broad chests. According to some experts, Patty in the Patterson-Gimlin film measures sixty inches around—and she was on the small side. The average sasquatch would measure sixty-five to seventy-five inches around. Male waists are said to taper more than female waists, although female hips are somewhat wider. Neither males nor females tend to have big bellies (except during pregnancy).

Their arms are very long and strong, and their slouch makes them look even longer. Some people report seeing hands hanging down around their knees. Those hands, of course, are also big and broader than human hands, although sasquatch fingers and especially their thumbs appear shorter and lack the thenar pad—that muscle at the base of your thumb. They have fingernails, not claws. Unsurprisingly, they have muscular legs, especially about the calves.

An actual bigfoot skeleton would tell a lot about how the creature came to be bipedal, and whether it followed a similar path to humans, or whether upright walking evolved independently. No bones about it, such a specimen would be a treasure for bigfoot enthusiasts.

A CLOSE-UP OF THE FOOT

If there's any one piece of bigfoot evidence that has excited people for decades, it's the footprint. The famous newspaper picture of Jerry Crew holding a big plaster cast made many people curious.

There's just one thing: How do we know the tracks are real?

It's true that thousands of footprints have been observed, and many have been cast in plaster and meticulously measured. It's also true that many of those reveal fingerprint-like ridges, scarring, and other things that leave some people convinced the tracks are real. For plenty of people, they are the consistent and compelling piece of evidence that makes sasquatch worth studying.

"Something is making those . . . tracks!" is what bigfoot searcher René Dahinden said about them. The search for their source was enough to

drive him to continue looking his whole life, even though it cost him his marriage and he died disappointed.

But there's one thing you can't get around. Without a bigfoot to use for comparisons and measurement, we don't know for sure what a bigfoot track looks like. There's just no way to avoid the fact that we're *assuming* these giant footprints that have been found all around the world are, in fact, bigfoot tracks. It is, after all, one possible explanation for them. The other is that they are all the result of hoaxes.

Of the two explanations, the former—that bigfoot left the tracks—is more persuasive to many people. How and why would so many hoaxers have left tracks? How would they independently create so many similar prints?

No matter what, there are several reasons to

study the tracks. For one thing, it's fun. What's more, it's a great way to learn about anatomy. And it's possible that we can make smart guesses about the rest of bigfoot's body—its size, its weight, the mechanics of its walk—using the footprints and what they reveal.

But there are limits to what the tracks can tell us. We have to remember two things: (1) that as scientific evidence, the tracks alone don't constitute proof that bigfoot is making them; and (2) anything we base on the tracks might not necessarily be correct, so we have to think of size and body projections as the best possible guess instead of as fact.

WHAT SOME OF THE BEST AND MOST FAMOUS TRACKS LOOK LIKE

In 1982, a Grays Harbor, Washington, Sheriff's deputy named Dennis Heryford took five notable casts of a fifteen-inch track. They're two inches wide and six inches deep, and they show features bigfoot seekers admire, including toenails and tendons, as well as dermal ridges and bunions. The tracks were found in clusters by more than one person, and they even had hair samples that Heryford sent to a laboratory for examination. One was found to belong to a human, but another had a "non-human root," and did not "resemble known human or primate hairs on file."

People who study these tracks believe they are evidence of an unknown animal. People who haven't seen the tracks for themselves often dismiss them, in part because hoaxers have been featured in the newspaper holding crudely carved molds they used to make fake tracks.

But many bigfoot tracks don't appear to have been made by a mold. Instead, they show what looks like a foot in motion. The toes are in different positions. The heel imprints are different depths. A partial imprint might indicate the sasquatch was running. Some tracks even show detail of the skin texture—fingerprint-like marks called dermatoglyphs—as well as healed scars.

Not all experts in bipedal walking agree on what the footprints signify. Some are of the mind that there is no bigfoot and all tracks are hoaxes. Others, though, like Professor Jeffrey Meldrum of Idaho State University, have pored over hundreds of tracks and made some fascinating observations about bigfoot feet. In a paper he wrote about alleged sasquatch footprints and how they might affect the creature's walk, he argued the following:

They are *not* enlarged human feet.

If you could put your feet in a magical enlarger and then leave a bunch of tracks on a muddy riverbank, the prints would be big, but not bigfoot prints. Bigfoot and human feet differ in several key ways:

Bigfoot has flat feet.

Human feet tend to have what's called a longitudinal arch. Unless you have flat feet, this means the bottom of your foot has an upward curve that runs from your foot's ball to its heel. You use your toes to push off from the ground when you're walking. Bigfoot feet don't work this way. Instead, a bigfoot foot has a more flexible midtarsal joint. In footprints, this shows up as a ridge across the footprint, created when the exceptionally bendy sasquatch foot presses the soil below it into a ridge.

Some bigfoot tracks have a "double ball."

On the inside of your own footprint, just below the toes, the ball of your foot curves out a bit. On bigfoot, there are sometimes two curves. This doesn't mean bigfoot has extra foot bones, but rather, that its flexible foot creases when it's bent. Bigfoot feet have thick pads of fat on their soles, which form this scallop shape. If you fold your hand in half, you might see the fleshy bit between your thumb and fingers do this same thing.

Bigfoot has long toes.

They're actually long, of course. They're also *relatively* long. In other words, they take up a bigger percentage of the overall foot than human toes do. Although they're longer in this way than human toes, they aren't as long as the toes of early bipedal hominid known as *Australopithecines*.

He is both spirit and real being,
but he can also glide through the forest,
like a moose with big antlers,
as though the trees weren't there.

— Oglala Lakota Medicine Man Pete Catches (as told to author Peter Matthiessen in the book *In the Spirit of Crazy Horse*)

SPOTTED!
"A Creature That Was Immensely Huge"

Chief Little Soldier lives on the Munsee Delaware Indian Reservation in Cambridge, Ohio. He's been aware of strange sights and sounds since 1998—occurrences that remind him of ancient stories told by his people.

He had his first sasquatch encounter when he was putting in trail markers. A branch broke. Something caught his eye.

"I saw a creature that was immensely huge looking back at me," he said. "It took off down the side of the ravine."

He gave chase, but had no hope of catching up with such a swift creature.

Making a sighting didn't scare him, though.

"It gave me a feeling of peace," he said. "It's kind of hard to explain, and it was kind of exciting at the same time."

BIGFOOT: A GRACEFUL CREATURE

Sasquatch has big feet, but it hasn't stopped the creature from moving with stunning grace, according to eyewitnesses. Instead of having bobbing heads, like human beings, they move with surprising smoothness.

As Bobo Fay puts it: "A common observation amongst witnesses when they see one, it looks like it's gliding like it's almost a human on a bicycle. You see the legs moving, but the shoulders and head hold fairly steady."

It might be smooth, but it's not a noiseless walk, according to Cliff Barackman. When a bigfoot roams the woods at night, it stirs up rodents, which attracts owls, he said. This is why bigfoot and owls are often found near each other. (Same with coyotes, who like to dine on sasquatch leftovers.)

It's also less like a human walk than you might think.

"The way a sasquatch walks seems to be very similar to a human being," Cliff explains. "But as it turns out, it's very different." Sasquatch footprints tend to line up in a "tightrope walk . . . one foot in front of the other."

They do this by swinging their leg out to the side and putting it down in front, something you can observe by watching the Patterson-Gimlin film. And instead of locking their knees, bigfoots are believed to keep them bent as they walk, minimizing their upper-body movement. Scientists call this a "compliant gait."

Jeffrey Meldrum, who specializes in the way animals move, has analyzed hundreds of suspected sasquatch footprints, comparing the shapes of the bones and the length of the toes and heels, to understand how bigfoot might walk and how it's different from a human walk.

People stride on stiff legs, striking the heel first and pushing off on the toe. We have relatively short toes that help propel us forward. Our feet are arched and not too flexible, leading to an efficient stride that doesn't tax the muscles too much.

Sasquatches, on the other hand, have flat, flexible feet and toes long enough to grab things. The flexibility of the foot helps propel a sasquatch forward (instead of the toes). From an evolutionary standpoint, it makes sense, Meldrum says.

"This would be an efficient strategy for negotiating the steep, broken terrain of the dense montane forests of the Pacific and Intermountain West, especially for a bipedal hominoid of considerable body mass," he writes in a report evaluating suspected sasquatch footprints and what they tell us about the way these creatures move. "The dynamic signatures of this adaptive pattern of gait are generally evident in the footprints examined in this study."

One thing that's up for debate is whether it's physically possible for humans to walk this way. If it's not, bigfoot-seekers argue, then the Patterson-Gimlin film couldn't possibly be a hoax.

Grover Krantz, the late professor of physical anthropology at Washington State University, said there was no way a person could walk like this. But Ranae Holland and others who've studied the subject disagree.

People can adopt a compliant gait when they aren't allowed to extend their knees or hips all the way as they walk. According to David Daegling, who wrote the book *Bigfoot Exposed,* people walking this way don't bob their hips, shoulders, and heads. And while you'd think you'd walk more slowly doing this, you can actually walk *faster.* The only catch is, it's tiring so you get worn out quickly. He tested this at Yale University, confirming it with a researcher at Duke University who studies the way people walk.

You can try it yourself—it's a walk many kids have been known to use when they are told not to run in the hallways at school. Or it's how you might walk if you were wearing a full diaper. In any case, it's safest to say that people *can* fake at least certain aspects of a bigfoot walk.

What's harder to explain are the eyewitness stories that describe bigfoot crossing a road in two steps, or the footprints that indicate a stride length outside the normal human range, and more within the range that a creature in the seven- to nine-foot range might make.

This is why it's worth it to keep looking, taking excellent care in your field notes to measure the distance between tracks, and to count how many steps it takes any bigfoots you witness to make it from one landmark to the next.

HOW THEY HUNT, WHAT THEY EAT

Unlike gorillas, chimpanzees, orangutans, and bonobos, bigfoots don't inhabit a tropical environment—at least not everywhere there have been sightings. In the mossy woods of the Pacific Northwest, for example, there's not a lot of edible plant matter. Certainly not enough to feed a creature this size.

But that's fine, bigfooters say. Unlike the gorilla, which is believed by most to exist on a great deal of fruit and plant matter, bigfoots are more like chimpanzees, which eat plants and meat.

Deer is a primary food source for the creatures, according to Matt Moneymaker. And bigfoot has a specific way of hunting, something noted by Mennonite farmers in eastern Ohio in the early 1990s. These creatures are believed to immobilize a deer by breaking one of its legs, Moneymaker says. That way, the animal can't run off.

"He breaks the leg and snaps it and twists it to disable it," Moneymaker says, "and then it pulls out the guts, the intestines, and goes after the liver."

This is why the *Finding Bigfoot* team pays special attention to deer carcasses it finds in the woods. If there's one with a foreleg that's been snapped clean and there's no other way to explain the injury, such as

tooth marks on the bone, it's a suspected sasquatch kill.

Depending on where a bigfoot lives, though, it might also eat crayfish, fish, or even duck.

"There's been a few instances that I know of for sure where squatches have come under geese and ducks and will swim under in a pond or a lake, come underneath them and just grab them—just yank them right down," Bobo Fay says.

Bigfoots aren't picky, as you might have guessed from the way they go after deer. They'll go after anything people leave out, including birdseed, cat food, and dog kibble.

Searchers step it up a bit when they're putting out bait. Favorite things to leave are piles of fruit and peanuts. But they'll even put out entire jars of peanut butter. And of course who can forget the bigfoot that is believed to have swiped a Zagnut bar, a candy made from peanut butter and toasted coconut? (See Chapter 5 for more about that incident.)

But that's not all. Bigfoot is believed to have a taste for a certain smoky breakfast staple.

"Bacon is a known squatch attractor," Bobo says. He likes to cook a bit when there's a light breeze going, "just to get the smell out."

Bobo always eats a piece first, to show any quietly observing sasquatches that he isn't out to poison them. Then he throws the rest into the bushes for any passing bigfoots to enjoy. You do have to be careful when you're using bacon bait. Bigfoot isn't the only creature that likes it—bears do, too.

SHARP SENSES

Dian Fossey and Jane Goodall are famous for their work observing gorillas and chimpanzees. These women were anything but overnight successes. In order to get close enough to these apes to study them, they had to track the creatures with great patience for months.

In part, it took this long just to start their research because apes see and hear much better than humans. Hearing is important in the jungle, where plants and vines make it hard to see things that are far away. This fine-tuned sense allowed Fossey's gorillas and Goodall's chimps to detect the scientists long before the scientists detected them—and it's likely that Goodall and Fossey finally got close to the animals once the animals were so accustomed to seeing them that they no longer cared to hide.

Bigfoot experts believe sasquatch hearing is similarly sharp.

"Sasquatches depend on their hearing to know where each other are at any given time," Cliff Barackman says. It's a communication and possibly warning system. "Sasquatches rely mostly on hearing to find if something is nearby, so it was trying to communicate something, possibly that we were there, to another sasquatch."

DO THE EYES HAVE IT?

Whether bigfoot sees in color would be a very interesting thing to determine. Scientists need to study an animal's actual eyes to know whether it can see in color. If an animal's eye has a type of cell called cones, then it should be able to see at least some colors.

Diurnal animals—ones that are awake during the day and asleep at night—tend to be the ones that see in color. Nocturnal primates—animals that are active at night and asleep during the day—don't have as much use for color vision. To understand why this is true, think about how

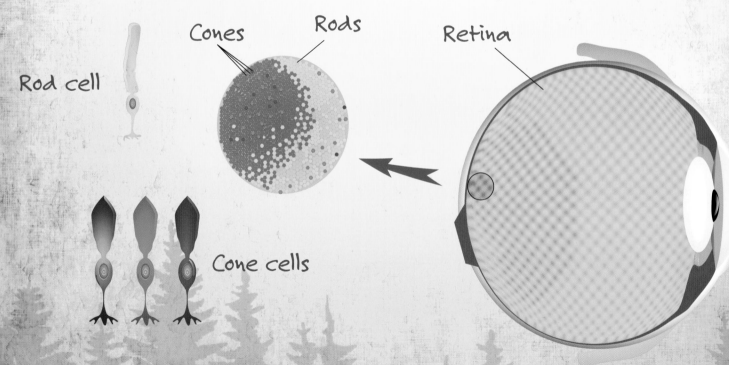

Rod cell

Cones

Rods

Retina

Cone cells

you see at night. Even if there's enough light to see a little bit, it's hard to tell what color things are. Your eyes need relatively bright light to pick out colors.

Humans and apes, which are diurnal, have eyes that allow for "trichromatic" vision. This means we have cones that let us distinguish between red, green, and blue (unless we're color-blind). Owl monkeys, the only truly nocturnal monkey species, have monochromatic vision. They can only see black and white and the gray tones in between.

So is bigfoot more like humans and apes, or more like nocturnal monkeys? It's hard to say. In truth, there aren't a lot of nocturnal primates. At best, we can only guess how bigfoot sees. And if the animals truly are nocturnal, chances are, bigfoot's world is black and white (and gray).

WHAT'S THAT SMELL?

According to the BFRO, about 10 to 15 percent of people who encounter bigfoot have been socked by a terrible odor. Gorillas have been known to produce a "fear smell" from certain underarm glands when they are threatened, so it's possible the sasquatch stench is a similar thing.

There's another aspect to smell, though—and that's how strong their sense of it is. Compared with humans, gorillas have a strong sense of smell. If you get sweaty walking through the jungle in search of a gorilla, it can smell you. Likewise, a male gorilla can tell by the smell when a female gorilla is ready to conceive a baby.

If a bigfoot's nose is like the next biggest ape's, chances are its nose knows people are near, which is perhaps why they're so elusive. They smell us coming and hide.

ENEMIES OF BIGFOOT

Bigfoot is an apex predator. This means it eats other animals, and that it doesn't have to worry a lot about being eaten by other animals, although it does share its habitat with bears, cougars, and other apex predators.

Threats to bigfoot are similar to threats to bears, cougars, wolves, and the like: other apex predators, including . . . humans. Although most people interested in bigfoot wouldn't dream of shooting one, there have been cases where people claimed to have done so.

Other dangers are development and environmental degradation, which is why it's important to preserve wild spaces and protect air and water quality in general. And then of course there's old age and disease, which will eventually take bigfoots that manage to survive other animals.

Making bigfoot calls can help lure the beasts out.

IS THEIR LANGUAGE REAL?

People who've had encounters with bigfoots have long reported consistent descriptions of the sounds the creatures make. It's a wide variety of noises, including screeches and howls, whistling sounds, and knocking noises. If you hear these noises when you're out squatching, one of the creatures might be nearby. If you hear another animal, though, it also might be a bigfoot because the animals are good mimics.

"They might imitate an owl. They could imitate a coyote, too. So even if that does sound very much like a coyote, it's possible that it was a bigfoot . . . imitating that to be able to call out to each other, while still trying to kind of mask their identity," Matt Moneymaker says. They do this to confuse whoever is in earshot.

SPOTTED!

A Hairy Go-Round at the Merry-Go-Round

It was 1984, and Lorena Cunningham was with her kids at a playground in Sharon, Ohio. Her children were sick of the swings and had just moved over to the merry-go-round when there was a crashing noise in the woods.

Lorena looked toward the sound. "This big, hairy creature was looking down at me," she said. "I was paralyzed with fright."

The seven- to eight-foot bigfoot she claims she saw experienced no such fear.

"It seemed to be at ease and curious," she said. "It was watching me and watching the children. It seemed to be interested. . . . I could see it looking at us."

Matt Moneymaker thinks Lorena might have seen a female sasquatch in this rare, daytime sighting. The she-squatch was curious about Cunningham's family.

BUT IS IT LANGUAGE?

It's one thing to make sounds. It's another thing to be capable of meaningful speech. Some people believe sasquatches do have their own language, though. One expert in 2010 transcribed what he calls the Sasquatch Phonetic Alphabet.

R. Scott Nelson, the author of this amazing alphabet, worked for many years as a military cryptologic linguist, which means he was responsible for listening to foreign communications (even coded ones), recognizing important signs, translating, and transcribing them. In short, he's an expert in recognizing language—even ones he doesn't speak. When his son was researching Bigfoot sounds for a school project, Nelson overheard a recording of the Sierra Sounds (see page 21) and recognized them as an actual language.

Intrigued, he spent a good deal of time listening to the sounds, observing, among other things, that sasquatches are fast talkers. Their speech flows at twice the rate of any known language.

Nelson devised the phonetic alphabet so listeners would have a consistent way to write down the sounds that are overheard. Eventually, this system might enable us to translate the sounds into language we understand (something he called "the recovery of the sasquatch language").

Nelson has advice if you overhear suspected sasquatch sounds. Record them in your field journal and be sure to keep track of the following:

- *how many bigfoots were present;*
- *how many were talking;*
- *whether they were talking to each other;*
- *what their emotional states seemed to be at each point in the conversation; and*
- *whether anything sounded like a question or a command.*

SPOTTED!
A Biologist and a Believer

Nick Maione, a Rhode Island biologist, was trekking through the state forest and working on his tracking skills. As he crawled along some rocks, he heard a snap.

"I looked—I saw a bigfoot. It went right around the corner," he said. "I mustered the courage, and I followed it."

He was close behind, only about one hundred twenty feet away, and he speculated that he'd woken the creature up from a nap, because until that moment, the woods had been silent, as had he.

The walking, bipedal creature made a great deal of noise but did not turn to look at Nick. Nonetheless, he's certain of what he saw.

"I'm a believer," he said. "This was a bigfoot."

DO OTHER ANIMALS HAVE LANGUAGE?

If sasquatch does have language, the creature won't be alone in this. Not only have certain animals learned to speak with humans, researchers believe many animals communicate with each other using languages native to their species.

ANIMALS THAT ARE FAMOUS FOR SPEAKING "HUMAN"

Koko the gorilla understands something like two thousand words in English. She can't speak them because her vocal cords aren't set up that way, but she can reply using some of the thousand American Sign Language gestures she knows. Including her own gorilla tongue, this means Koko knows three languages, which she uses to communicate things as abstract as emotions. (Another gorilla she lived with, Michael, knew six hundred words.) And she's quite a talker. She initiates most conversations with the humans who work with her, and can put together statements made of three to six words.

An African gray parrot named Alex, meanwhile, learned one hundred fifty words. The night before he died at age thirty-one, he told his handler, "You be good. See you tomorrow. I love you." He was also a crack mathematician who could count up to eight and add sums up to six, in addition to being able to put numbers in order from one through eight using labels in English.

THE CHALLENGES IN TRANSLATING "ANIMAL"

Scientists are trying hard to decode the languages used by many species, including dolphins, elephants, wolves, and chimps. It's no easy thing, though. Dolphins, for example, make all sorts of sounds, including clicks and whistles. One theory holds that they use a "sonopictorial" language, which embeds images into sound waves. When the waves bounce off objects, the dolphins understand the images being expressed in sound. Researchers at speakdolphin.com created a device that makes sound waves visible, and found that dolphins could recognize images broadcast 86 percent of the time.

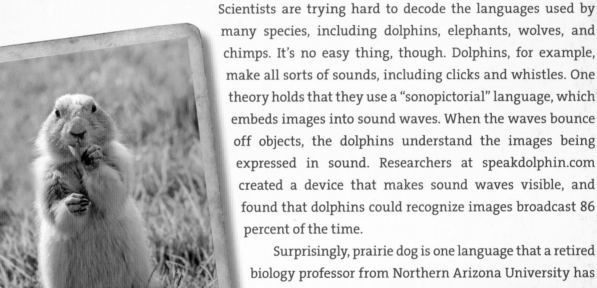

Surprisingly, prairie dog is one language that a retired biology professor from Northern Arizona University has succeeded in cracking. Constantine Slobodchikoff, the professor, has reported that prairie dogs give each other detailed warning calls when a potential predator is near. For example, they say something different when a heavy, tall human in a blue T-shirt is near than they do when a short, thin person in green approaches.

Chapter Nine
BIGGEST BIGFOOT HOAXES

Not every fake bigfoot or yeti sighting is a hoax. For example, in March of 1986, an experienced hiker was in the Himalayas when he saw a creature with a "large and squarish" head and a dark body covered in hair. It didn't move. He also observed a line of strange tracks that appeared to lead up to this mysterious animal. He photographed it, and bigfoot experts who analyzed it concluded it was a genuine, undoctored picture of a yeti.

The hiker, Anthony Woolridge, was experienced and would know what he'd seen, so people were eager to believe him. But the next year, when researchers went back to the spot to do more investigation, they found the yeti was actually a rock outcropping.

This was a case of a mistake. No one was trying to trick anyone else. But people really wanted to believe Woolridge had seen a yeti, and so they did. If such a thing can happen accidentally, consider how much more susceptible people are to believing hoaxes—people's intentional attempts to trick others into believing something.

These pranks might seem funny at the time, but most people don't end up laughing for long. Someone tramping through the woods in a bigfoot suit could accidentally get shot by a hunter. In 2012, a man wearing a kind of hairy-looking camouflage costume called a Ghillie suit was hit by two cars driven by teenagers in Montana. His friends told police he was trying to make people think they'd seen a sasquatch. Tragically, he died.

Ghillie suits, like this one, make you undetectable.

It's also cruel to mislead and waste the time of people who've devoted their lives to finding bigfoot. They take this work seriously. Imagine how you would feel if someone took the thing that meant the most to you and turned it into a joke. It also ruins the credibility of a group of people who really are trying to investigate something scientifically.

There is one thing about bigfoot, though, that stands separate from all the hoaxes. John Green, the journalist who spent his career seeking the animal, said, "If you establish at any point that even one report is accurate, then you have an animal. And, if you have an animal, then you have literally thousands of animals."

In other words, people can pull all the bigfoot hoaxes they want. If we someday find an animal, then bigfoot exists—and there can't be just one.

CARDIFF GIANT

While no one claimed the Cardiff Giant was bigfoot (the term hadn't been invented yet), when this ten-foot stone man was "discovered" on October 16, 1869, in Cardiff, New York, he became a truly big deal. Thousands of people traveled to a farm to pay fifty cents each to see the stone colossus, which was said to be an example of the giants referred to in the Bible.

Some people were fooled. A journalist describing the effect the giant had on some onlookers said it took their breath away and made them look awestruck. No matter how it affected these early witnesses, this stone man wasn't a real giant. It was a sculpture made by stonecutters. A tobacco salesman named George Hull had paid the stonecutters and the farmer a total of $2,600 to create and house the giant.

Hull had taken some pains with his project.

He found the stone in Montana and paid to ship it to Chicago, where stonecutters set to work, using Hull's body as their model. It was fairly detailed (you could see ribs and other bits), and Hull himself used a sponge, water, and sand to make the giant look as though he were an ancient being.

Hull's efforts to make his giant seem real were for nothing—at least from a scientific standpoint. A paleontologist from Yale University inspected it and pronounced it an obvious hoax because the chisel marks were visible.

But something surprising happened after this: People didn't care. They kept paying to see it.

The fake giant became so popular that P. T. Barnum, the circus owner who allegedly said, "There's a sucker born every minute," had a plaster copy made. That one became even more popular than the original.

This just shows how much people want to believe in fantastic things. Even when presented with evidence to the contrary, they'll still go along with it—just for fun.

Oh, and about that P. T. Barnum quote about suckers? He never said it. It's just another thing people like to believe.

THE MINNESOTA ICEMAN

In the late 1960s and early 1970s, a retired Air Force pilot named Frank Hansen had something pretty cool in his trailer: a frozen wild man dubbed "The Minnesota Iceman." Hansen took it to carnivals and fairs, charging people a quarter for a peek.

It's not clear where Hansen got his supposed sasquatch. At a critical moment, the story kept changing. . . .

It came from a rich, mysterious owner!

It was discovered in the seas of Siberia!

It attacked him in the woods and he killed it in self-defense!

But before all that, when the frozen wild man was entertaining Midwestern fairgoers, Bernard Heuvelmans, the father of cryptozoology, examined it for a period of days with Ivan Sanderson, the founder of the ABSMery. Impressed, these two notables were ready to declare it real. Not only did Sanderson say he could smell it rotting through the cracks in the ice, Heuvelmans was ready to identify it as a previously unknown species.

His name for the creature was *Homo pongoides*, and the way he described it in *The*

Bulletin of the Royal Institute of Natural Sciences of Belgium was convincing. The wild man they nicknamed Bozo looked like a six-foot-tall man covered from head to toe in hair, he wrote. His skin was waxy white and cadaverish, like a Caucasian man who hadn't seen much sun. His broken left arm was twisted behind his head, while his right lay against his body, the palm pressed against his belly.

But it was Bozo's face that was most surprising, Sanderson wrote in a magazine called *Argosy*. Both eyes seemed to be missing. One was blown out. Bozo had a wide, flat nose, "rather like that of a Pekinese dog." Sanderson was insistent the thing was real. "Then again, you may well be able to fool me, I fully admit," he wrote. "But I defy anybody to fool Bernard Heuvelmans in a case like this."

Sanderson asked John Napier at the Smithsonian to investigate, and this is when things took a strange turn. Hansen's story about the origins of the creature changed. Then he took a "vacation," and during that time, someone allegedly replaced the original Iceman with a

fake made out of latex. The Smithsonian weighed in harshly after their investigation turned up the company that had made just such a suit for Hansen.

"The Smithsonian Institution . . . is satisfied that the creature is simply a carnival exhibit made of latex rubber and hair . . . the 'original' model and the present so-called 'substitute' are one and the same."

And so ended the saga. Or so everyone thought. Early in 2013, someone claiming to have the rubber suit put it and a nonworking freezer up for sale on eBay with an asking price of $20,000. It sold—for how much, they don't say. Nor do they say where the suit is going, so the mystery might live on a while longer.

SQUATCHCICLE, PART II

In 2008, a couple of guys in Georgia—later joined by a Las Vegas promoter—created the biggest bigfoot hoax in modern times, again with what they claimed was a frozen sasquatch.

A press release sent to reporters beforehand promised DNA evidence and photos of the beast. Judging by some of the claims in the press release, it's no wonder many people were excited. They claimed they'd found a seven-foot seven-inch creature that weighed more than five hundred pounds, looked part human and part ape, was male with reddish hair and blackish-gray eyes, and was in possession of two arms, two legs, and the usual number of fingers and toes. Its feet measured sixteen and three-quarters inches long, and were flat and human-like. And it was an upright walker (as were the other specimens sighted the day this one was discovered).

So where'd they get it? According to their tall tale, the two men, Matthew Whitton and Rick Dyer, had been on a June hike in the woods of Georgia when a creature began to follow them. In all, they saw three other bigfoot-like creatures before they found the prize, the body of a seven-foot-seven sasquatch near a stream. Tom Biscardi, the Vegas promoter, said he'd inspected the body before it was frozen and was certain it was authentic, according to the *National Geographic* news Web site.

Some people's flags went up right away, because Biscardi had been involved in an earlier bigfoot hoax. But Whitton was especially persuasive because he was a police officer on leave from his job as he recovered from being shot in the hand while he arrested someone, which is probably why reporters from respected media outlets, including CNN, went to the infamous press conference on August 15, 2008.

Whitton pretended the whole thing had been a happy accident. "We were not looking for bigfoot . . . we wouldn't know what we were doing if we did," he said. "I didn't believe in bigfoot at the time . . . but you've got to come to terms with it and realize you've got something special. And that's what it was."

They even showed reporters photographs of a sasquatch that had been allegedly following them.

Although there were skeptics all along, lots of people were very excited to see the creature.

Loren Coleman, a well-known cryptozoologist, posted pictures on the cryptomundo blog a few days before the press release. The photos depict a chocolate-brown, furry beast with white teeth and a protruding tongue. They also reveal a knot of pale pink guts on the creature's belly.

He wrote, "The body doesn't look exactly like people thought it would, because the Patterson-Gimlin bigfoot has been the model in our minds. However, this looks as if it is an actual apelike primate. Indeed, the gorilla-like facial features, the alleged lack of canines, and the grinding surfaces shown in the teeth *suggest* a bulky vegetarian with a mixture of higher primate characteristics."

You can hear the mix of optimism and

SPOTTED!

"I'd Never Seen Anything Like It Before"

Kirsten Jorgensen was cranking tunes on her Game Boy as she took a quick trip down the hill to the mailbox. That's when she noticed something out of the corner of her eye. The Virginia teen turned to look, "and I was, like, 'Oh my gosh! There's something standing there watching me.'"

She ran up the hill screaming. As soon as she got to the house, she caught her breath and burst into tears. "I'd never seen anything like it before."

skepticism in that post. Afterward, on an entry outlining many more details of the ways Biscardi in particular had tried to trick him, Coleman wrote, "I was ninety-nine percent sure this was a hoax. However, I honestly admitted that I had a tiny bit of hope that perhaps some of the most unreliable people around had come up with a body."

Other scientifically minded bigfoot hunters were turned off immediately. Matt Moneymaker told *Scientific American* that the pictures looked like "a Halloween costume in a box." Jeffrey Meldrum, the professor at Idaho State University, said pretty much the same thing, and that his previous contact with Biscardi made the whole thing seem made-up.

THE RAY WALLACE SAGA

When Ray Wallace died in 2002, *The Seattle Times* wrote an article that said, "The reality is, bigfoot just died."

The reporter was quoting Ray Wallace's son, Michael, who claimed his father had made the original tracks in 1958 that Jerry Crew discovered—the very tracks that made bigfoot a household name in the United States.

Wallace couldn't help himself, his relatives said. "He'd been a kid all his life. He did it just for the joke and then he was afraid to tell anybody because they'd be so mad at him," his nephew Dale Lee Wallace said.

For sure, Wallace did some things that make him *seem* like a prankster. For example, in 1960 he claimed to have caught a young bigfoot. He offered it to Peter Byrne for a million dollars. Byrne, who led several bigfoot-seeking expeditions in the Pacific Northwest, counter-offered $5,000 for a peek. They couldn't make a deal. Later, Wallace told Byrne the baby bigfoot was eating him into the poorhouse (his food of choice: Kellogg's Frosted Flakes by the hundred-pound bag), but he never did get the money and claims to have released the animal.

He moved from California to Toledo, Washington, where he ran a roadside zoo and entertained himself by writing fifty-page letters to his old hometown newspaper, the *Klamity Kourier*, detailing tales of bigfoots who befriended cougars, spoke in their own language, and lived in abandoned gold mines. He also made bigfoot movies and took supposed pictures of the creature in the wild, eating elk and frogs, among other things.

One of his claims to the newspaper: "Bigfoot used to be very tame, as I have seen him almost every morning on the way to work," he wrote in 1969. "I would sit in my pickup and toss apples out of the window to him. He never did catch an apple, but he sure tried."

After his death, his family produced a pair of carved alder wood feet—the ones they said gave life to the whole bigfoot myth. And for a lot of people, that was proof enough that there is no bigfoot.

There's just one problem, though. Most bigfoot tracks that have been cast don't match those wooden templates, so anyone dismissing bigfoot on the basis of Ray Wallace's family confessions is missing out on a great deal of research. It's possible that he was a hoaxer *and* that there is also such an animal we think of as bigfoot.

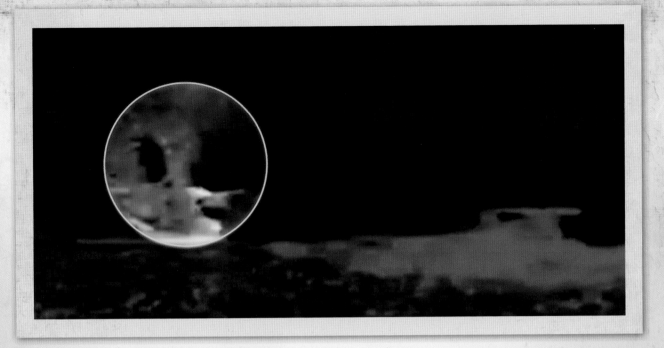

RANT MULLENS

One of the earliest bigfoot hoaxers might just be a man named Rant Mullens, who claimed he started fooling people with giant footprints in 1924, long before the name "bigfoot" was even coined.

In that early incident, a gold miner named Fred Beck said that apes armed with rocks had attacked his camp. The *Portland Oregonian* carried an article about the "Ape Canyon" incident, which Beck later described at length. Beck and his crew had seen mysterious tracks during their work. "We knew no known animal could have made them: The largest measured nineteen inches long."

They considered leaving, but everyone was excited about the prospect of finding gold, so they soldiered on. And then one night, their cabin came under attack. Someone or something was pelting them with rocks. The attack lasted all night. In the morning, when things ended, Beck looked outside.

"It was not long before I saw one of the ape-like creatures, standing about eighty yards away near the edge of Ape Canyon. I shot three times, and it toppled over the cliff, down into the gorge, some four hundred feet below."

Was it a bigfoot attack?

Well, fast-forward fifty-eight years to when Rant Mullens took credit for the Ape Canyon attack. There are persuasive photographs of him showing feet he carved. He also admitted to providing similar ones to Ray Wallace, who was linked to the Bluff Creek Bigfoot tracks that inspired many people to seek bigfoot. And he said he sold fake feet for fifty years, any of which could be still out there, being used.

But knowing there are guys like Rant Mullens out there doesn't deter experts like Jeffrey Meldrum. He's spent his career studying footprints and, in the real ones, he sees things that could only be made by a living foot interacting with the soil beneath.

CRAZY CLAIMS

You'll remember that science follows certain rules. For something to be a scientific theory, you need to be able to make observations. You need to turn these observations into a hypothesis— an educated guess about something. You need to test this hypothesis with an experiment that proves or disproves your hypothesis, and that other people can repeat. This part is vital, and it's why certain ideas about bigfoot have been unhelpful in advancing understanding of the creature.

In the 1980s, for example, a woman named B. Ann Slate cowrote a book with one of the men who recorded the Sierra Sounds. In part, the book considered the possibility that bigfoot might be an advance guard for an incoming alien invasion. It's an, uh, interesting idea. But how on earth would one test it? The idea continues to circulate today. A cable TV host, Dr. Franklin Ruehl, has written for *The Huffington Post* making the same case (and you can watch him on YouTube saying, "May bigfoot be with you. Yes! Yes! Yes!").

Another man with unusual ideas, Jon-Erik Beckjord, had a similarly unprovable theory that explained why no one had ever managed to kill a sasquatch, and why they were so hard to spot. It's because they live "between dimensions" and can fade out through wormholes, possibly to parallel universes.

SPOTTED!
The Last Hunting Trip

Jeff Boling, a police officer and hunter from southwest Virginia, was up before dawn walking along a ridge when he heard something coming through the high grass.

"I could tell it was like a man," he said, describing the serpentine path it made alongside him. Eventually, it walked out of earshot—and into plain view. That's when he realized it wasn't a man after all. It was a bigfoot. His life hasn't been the same since.

"It was November of 1993," he said, "and to this day, I have not hunted anymore."

THE CRIPPLEFOOT CONUNDRUM

One of the most confounding episodes in bigfoot history has to be the "Cripplefoot" incident, because it's a mix of the believable and the nutty, the rational and the rascally.

In November 1969, a butcher near the small eastern Washington town of Bossburg found some mysterious tracks near a garbage dump. People had been spotting sasquatches in the area, so the tracks were an instant source of curiosity. And they were interesting: One foot looked messed up, possibly drawing bigfoot close to people and their castoffs because it could not survive in the wild.

Before long, some of the most notable names in bigfoot history had gathered to study the tracks: René Dahinden, Bob Titmus, and Ivan Marx (who lived nearby). After the initial discovery of tracks, they did their best to find more—or the creature that made them. A few weeks later, they came upon a series of 1,089 tracks in the snow. More experts arrived, including Roger Patterson. They searched without luck into January, all the while wondering if the tracks were a hoax.

Things started to get strange after that. A local prospector said he'd trapped a live bigfoot in an abandoned mineshaft. He at first offered to sell it. Later, he offered to sell a frozen sasquatch foot. (No one ever saw either.) After that, Ivan Marx produced what he claimed was footage of the Cripplefoot after it was hit by a train. His claim was undermined, though, by reports that he'd been seen shopping for fur earlier that month in Spokane, Washington. The footage also didn't hold up to scrutiny.

But here's the kicker.

The tracks themselves were convincing to experts, including Professor Grover Krantz, John Napier of the Smithsonian, and later, to Jeffrey Meldrum, the professor at Idaho State University.

Meldrum wrote that you could see evidence of movement in the tracks. "In some instances, the toes are sharply curled, leaving an undisturbed ridge of soil behind toe tips resembling peas in a pod. In other instances the toes are fully extended," he wrote in a paper analyzing them.

This isn't the sort of thing you'd expect a hoaxer to do, or to even know was possible. In Napier's book, *Bigfoot: The Yeti and Sasquatch in Myth and Reality*, he wrote, "It is very difficult to conceive of a hoaxer so subtle, so knowledgeable—and so sick—who would deliberately fake a footprint of this nature. I suppose it's possible, but it is so unlikely that I am prepared to discount it."

And Krantz was even more emphatic when he talked with a television reporter. "If someone faked [these footprints] with all the subtle hints of anatomy design, he had to be a real genius, an expert at anatomy, very inventive, an original thinker. He had to outclass me in those areas, and I don't think anyone outclasses me in those areas, at least not since Leonardo da Vinci. So I say such a person is impossible, therefore the tracks are real."

PAUL FREEMAN

Paul Freeman is a controversial figure in the bigfoot world. He found many, many tracks. The one-time U.S. Forest Service worker also captured suspected bigfoot video. But old-school bigfooters like Titmus and Dahinden thought he was nothing but a hoaxer.

He gained a certain respectability, though, when scholars like Krantz and Meldrum took serious interest in the bigfoot casts he tracked. Meldrum was initially skeptical. But when he went out to look at some tracks in the Blue Mountains area of southeastern Washington, he was blown away. The line of prints he observed in wet, silty soil had all the characteristics of prints made by a living foot.

"These are all the features that make it come to life in my mind and began to cause me to set aside my skepticism," he told a reporter for the *Yakima Herald*. "While it's clearly from the same foot, in one instance the toes are tightly flexed and it's gripping the soil on a slight incline . . . in one extended and splayed, the first three toes sunken into the soil but the fourth and fifth don't quite leave a mark."

One print even showed a rock that had pressed into the soft sole of the foot. Another showed how the creature's toes had wrapped around a larger rock. Meldrum cast the prints, ready to conclude they were still a hoax. Later, an expert in primate handprints examined the casts and found scars and dermal ridges. The expert, Jimmy Chilcutt, concluded they were real—and belonged to a mysterious, nonhuman primate.

SPOTTED!
Moonshine and Bigfoot

Brandon and Leslie White have an old cabin in the mountains of Kentucky. It's remote—surrounded by a thousand acres of wilderness—the perfect place to slow-cook ribs and raccoon, play bluegrass tunes on the fiddle, and maybe even brew up some moonshine, a potent kind of liquor made of fermented cornmeal.

Everything changes at night, though. That's when the sasquatches come out.

"In the middle of the night they come around here knocking and banging," Brandon said. "You can hear them, I don't know, it sounds like they're kind of talking. But it ain't nothing I ever heard before."

But it doesn't end with bigfoot banter.

"They throw rocks," Leslie said. A couple of times a month, the cabin is pelted.

HOW TO SPOT A FAKER

The history of bigfoot hoaxes can teach us a few things. For example, if someone is offering to sell you peeks at a bigfoot, a captured bigfoot, or bigfoot body parts, you're wise to be suspicious. Real bigfooters are interested in finding the animal for the sake of science, not profit. It's a question of credibility, which is diminished when people are obviously out for a buck.

The same thing applies when the *Finding Bigfoot* team interviews witnesses. They ask questions designed to make sure the witnesses can be trusted. If the alleged bigfoot that's been spotted isn't behaving in a typically squatchy way, that makes the story seem less credible. Similarly suspicious are bigfoot tracks that are uniform or spaced incorrectly—a bigfoot walks in a single-file gait and has a step length of around five feet.

There are also telltale clues with videos that alert them to hoaxes. Genuine videos aren't short, Bobo Fay says. If a video is just a couple of seconds, if it's shaky, if it includes just a quick pan of some creature, it's probably a hoax.

"When it's a real video, people keep filming. When they're kind of, like, trying to keep it as brief as possible, that's an indicator sign for a possible hoax."

You also want to see telltale sasquatch signs when you're looking at a video, Cliff Barackman says. Is the posture right for a squatch? Does it have butt muscles? It should, he says, "because that's a physical trait that is absolutely necessary for bipedal walking."

That said, even hoax videos are worth studying. Matt Moneymaker puts it like this: "Investigating potentially hoax videos is important also because you can't become an expert on bigfoot videos unless you become very familiar with both legit footage and hoax footage."

Chapter Ten
EXTRAS

Certain questions about bigfoot come up again and again. Here are answers to the most common of them.

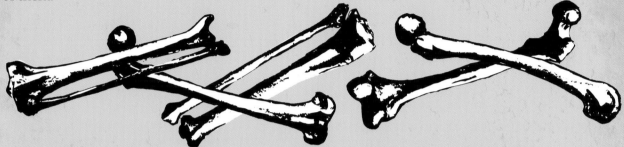

WHERE ARE THE BIGFOOT BONES?

A bigfoot skeleton—or even part of one—could be used as proof of the animal's existence. So far, though, no one has come forward with any bones. People who reject the possibility of bigfoot use this as an argument for their cause. No bones, no bigfoot.

Not so fast, though, bigfooters argue. For one thing, fossils are very rare, particularly in wet environments like Washington State, where many of the sightings have been made. For another thing, bigfoots themselves are rare, with perhaps only two to six thousand in all of North America, according to estimates of the Bigfoot Field Researchers Organization. For someone to stumble across exceedingly rare bigfoot remains in a remote part of the world would also be an unlikely event, especially given Mother Nature's propensity to absorb dead animals back into the soil, assisted by animals such as porcupines, which eat bones.

But the main reason we haven't found bigfoot bones is that we haven't been looking for them, the BFRO says. "No one should expect remains of such an elusive species to be found, collected, and identified without some effort."

HOW DID BIGFOOT GET HERE FROM THE HIMALAYAS?

We don't know for sure that's where bigfoot came from, although it is a logical theory, for a couple of really good reasons:

First, we know that Asia was home to giant apes. One species in particular, *Gigantopithecus blacki*, is often offered up as a potential bigfoot relative.

Second, we also know that during the last Ice Age, between 70,000 and 11,000 years ago, a land bridge connected Asia and North America. This is how early humans made their way to the New World. If bigfoot *is* related to Asian apes, this would be the most reasonable means of getting to North America.

HOW MANY BIGFOOTS ARE OUT THERE?

No one knows for sure. But the Bigfoot Field Researchers Organization estimates there are between two thousand and six thousand bigfoots in North America.

The animals are only rarely spotted, which means—no surprise—that they're rare. But there needs to be a certain number of them to sustain the population. The BFRO thinks about three hundred would be a minimum.

But there have been many more sightings than that, so the number is probably higher. When wildlife biologists are trying to gauge the size of an animal population, they use a principle called the "observability factor." For every single animal you see, there might be four others of the same species. That would give you an observability factor of four to one.

What's the observability factor for bigfoot? It's hard to say for sure, but the BFRO estimates based on the four thousand credible sightings recorded since the 1960s, it's reasonable to guess at their two to six thousand bigfoot figure. Grover Krantz, a professor of physical anthropology, concurred, basing his population estimate in the "low thousands" on the number of prints that had been collected and the average life expectancy of a sasquatch.

SPOTTED!
A Lightbulb Moment

Rosie Caldwell was on the porch of her Kentucky home, making a phone call in the dark. She wasn't happy about it.

"I'm a scaredy cat," she said, "so I went to turn the porch light on."

But it wasn't working. So she fetched a bulb, and as she was changing it, she saw something.

"I saw a huge, seven- to eight-foot creature just strolling by," she said. "It turned and looked at me while it was walking." The creature had sloped shoulders and it swung its arms as it moved.

Terrified, she dropped everything and ran into the basement. "After I got in the house," she said, "I called my dad."

"I think I saw a bigfoot," she told him.

He rushed over. They went to look for it, but whatever mysterious creature she'd seen had disappeared right into the woods.

HOW MANY TYPES OF BIGFOOTS ARE THERE?

Without having even a single bigfoot specimen to examine, no one can say for sure if the creature is the same as the Florida Skunk Ape, the Himalayan Yeti, the Indonesian Orang Pendek, or the Australian Yowie.

Given the distance that separates the Pacific Northwest from Florida, Nepal, Indonesia, and Australia, though, as well as the differences in the creatures' appearances and behaviors that witnesses have described, it would be reasonable to expect them to be different species, at least.

HOW AGGRESSIVE ARE THEY?

Before people knew much about gorillas, the animals had a reputation of being aggressive, chest-thumping menaces. In reality, their nickname among wildlife biologists is "gentle giants."

We haven't been able to observe sasquatches as closely, but in all of the thousands of sightings in the past sixty years or so, there hasn't been a single human death or serious injury caused by bigfoot. Compared with other apex predators, bigfoots seem downright tame. For example, since 1890, twenty people have been killed by cougars in North America. Bears are even deadlier. Since 2000, thirty-four people have been killed by either black or brown bears.

WHAT DOES BIGFOOT EAT?

Bigfoot is an omnivore, which means it eats plants and other animals. Wherever it lives, it needs protein and water. In the Pacific Northwest, deer, elk, and rodents are sources of protein. In Florida, the skunk ape is believed to eat deer and wild hogs, as well as snakes, alligators, and swamp apples.

Many bigfooters put out bait for the animals, hoping to get a peek. Favorite bait items include bacon, raw liver, peanut butter, and candy bars, which means bigfoot and truck drivers like the same foods (just kidding—we aren't up on our truck driver research).

IS THERE TRUE EVIDENCE THAT IT EVEN EXISTS?

There is evidence but not proof. Evidence has been found in the form of footprints, hair, scat, and encounters—some of which have been recorded in pictures and video. People don't always agree on their interpretations of this evidence, but there is evidence for sure. To have proof of bigfoot, we would need a body or part of a body. To date, that has not happened.

IS BIGFOOT AS BROWN AS A BEAR?

Eyewitnesses have described seeing bigfoot with all sorts of different hair colors—black, brown, reddish—even gray and white streaks in more senior sasquatches. Their skin is dark, either brown or black, although it's lighter on their palms and soles, witnesses have reported.

HOW TALL IS A SASQUATCH?

When it comes to determining the average size for humans, researchers can simply measure a number of people and work it out from there. There are complications—some populations are taller than others. But there are people readily available for measurement.

It's not so with sasquatches. So how did researchers come up with seven foot ten as the average height of a bigfoot? Two ways: using landmarks for measurements, and making projections based on the size of their feet.

Seven foot ten is the average, though. Some are even taller. Based on footprint size, the biggest are believed to top ten feet.

They are correspondingly heavy. As height increases, weight goes up *exponentially*, because the volume of the body is greater. Think of it this way. A cube measuring two feet on a side has a volume of eight. A cube measuring three feet on a side has a volume of twenty-seven. The average squatch tips the scales at six hundred fifty pounds. Jumbos might weigh over a thousand pounds, based on some of the largest footprints.

Here's James "Bobo" Fay demonstrating
the massive height of bigfoot.

SPOTTED!
"It Was Built Like . . . a Rock"

Phil Ramos was hunting in the Morgan-Monroe State Park, a 24,000-acre tract in southern Indiana. He sat by a tree for a moment and heard a twig snap. His hunter's instincts kicked in. He spotted its massive head and shoulders, trained his gun on it, and watched it follow the tree lines before cutting into the woods.

"I got a good look at it. It was tall. I would say at least ten, twelve feet," he said. "It was built like . . . a rock." Scared stiff at the time, he told no one of the sighting but his wife. And he never went back to that spot in the woods.

After Bobo visited the spot, he was a believer. "After being at the site with Phil and having him recount his story, relive his story, there's no doubt in my mind this dude is . . . telling the truth. This guy really saw and experienced what he says he did. I believe the guy a hundred percent."

HOW DOES SASQUATCH SURVIVE IN THE MOUNTAINS?

Like any wild animal, sasquatches are adapted to survive in the habitats where they've been seen. As with other apex predators, they feed on smaller animals. As omnivores, they also eat plants. They also need water.

IS SASQUATCH CURIOUS?

Many sasquatch sightings describe the animals peering into windows, visiting barns, and investigating loud sounds such as chainsaws, explosions, and playing children. Some have even been said to observe humans for hours. For the most part, though, their curiosity seems balanced by their desire to remain hidden away.

For sure, humans are more curious about sasquatches than they are about us.

HOW LONG DO THEY LIVE?

Gorillas in the wild live about thirty-five to forty years. In captivity, they live a bit longer—up to fifty years or so. Writing for the International Society of Cryptozoology in 1998, W. Henner Fahrenbach calculated a similar life expectancy based on the size of a sasquatch and its nine-month gestation period. Some animals do live longer, he wrote. Those are the old-looking creatures that people have reported seeing, old and wrinkled with rotten teeth and hair that looks like "goat dreadlocks."

WHAT CLIMATE DOES BIGFOOT PREFER?

Judging by where Bigfoot is most often seen, the thickly forested, temperate rain forests of Washington State are their favorite habitat. Almost 13 percent of all sightings occur there. That said, sightings have been reported in every state except for Hawaii. No sightings have been made in Washington, D.C., either.

WOULD BIGFOOT EAT A HUMAN?

There are no reports of human consumption by bigfoot. President Teddy Roosevelt wrote a book that contained a story of a fatal attack by a sasquatch-like animal, but even then, the victim—who had a broken neck—wasn't eaten. Or even nibbled on.

HOW MANY PEOPLE HAVE SEEN BIGFOOT?

No one knows! But the Bigfoot Field Researchers Organization database lists more than 4,300 sightings. Almost certainly there are many more than that. Not everyone who sees bigfoot reports it to the database. And many people who see bigfoot never tell anyone, because they're afraid of being ridiculed.

WHAT PERCENTAGE OF AMERICANS BELIEVE IN BIGFOOT?

An Angus Reid Public Opinion poll in 2012 found that almost 30 percent of Americans believe in bigfoot. Democrats are more likely to say bigfoot is "probably real," and men are more likely than women to believe.

30% BELIEVE

70% DON'T BELIEVE

WHAT DO YOU DO IF YOU SEE A BIGFOOT?

Remember that bigfoot is a wild animal. Staring at wild animals can be perceived as threatening, so as tempting as it might be to goggle away, it would be better for you to sit down and look unthreatening. Have a snack. Pretend to pick fleas out of your friend's hair.

Then, slowly remove your camera if you have one and slyly snap some pictures or capture video. Do your best to make observations and not scare it off, and then write a really great entry in your field journal.

IS IT A BOY OR A GIRL?

We talk about "Bigfoot" as though there is just one. But of course, there couldn't possibly be just one. A bigfoot can be male or female. One of the most famous—the one in the Patterson-Gimlin film—had female body parts. Her fans named her Patty.

WAS BIGFOOT EVER CAPTURED ON FILM?

Some of the best evidence for bigfoot is on film (go back and look at Chapter 2, if you haven't). So, yes. There are plenty of people who believe they have photographed and filmed bigfoot. The most famous of all bigfoot films is the Patterson-Gimlin film (see page 18). It has been reviewed many times by experts and no one has proved it authentic or faked, although there are people who firmly believe it's one or the other.

You can look up the movie on YouTube and decide for yourself. There's also a Facebook group called FB/FB (for Facebook/Find Bigfoot), and people there analyze footage. They've posted many, many videos and photographs.

IS CHEWBACCA A BIGFOOT?

Chewbacca was a Wookiee, and while he certainly looks like a bigfoot and talks like a bigfoot, he isn't—at least according to George Lucas, who created the character.

He also said the name Wookiee came from a line one of his actors made up during the shooting of *THX 1138*, a sci-fi movie that came before *Star Wars*: "I think I just wan over a wookiee on the expressway."

But the personality of Chewbacca is based on Lucas's loyal, brave dog, Indiana.

HOW DOES BIGFOOT MOVE AROUND WITHOUT BEING SPOTTED?

There have been some wackadoodle theories about that. One of the most outlandish is that bigfoot travels through wormholes to other dimensions.

More reasonable theories: bigfoot is nocturnal. Humans aren't equipped to see particularly well at night. Bigfoots are also rare and live in remote areas, two other factors that make them harder to see. As with many animals, they will have evolved characteristics that camouflage them—dark fur that blends in with the shadows of the forest, for example.

And, some researchers believe, they don't want to be seen. Jeffrey Meldrum, author of *Sasquatch: Legend Meets Science,* said there is evidence that chimpanzees obscure their tracks and take other measures to avoid detection. Perhaps bigfoot does the same.

HAVE A BIGFOOT MOVIE NIGHT

Let's say you and your friends are into bigfoot, big-time. After a long day of research, you can unwind together with any number of famous bigfoot movies while you eat Zagnut bars.

Here are some you might like.

Legend of Boggy Creek

This movie, from the early 1970s, is a docu-drama—it's meant to look real. This is definitely the most famous of all bigfoot movies, and it is based on events that really happened in Fouke, Arkansas, where a smelly, seven-foot monster was killing chickens and scaring people half to death. (There's a sequel called *Boggy Creek II: And the Legend Continues*.)

Harry and the Hendersons

For a bit more comedy, this movie is about a man who runs into bigfoot (literally), brings him home, discovers him to be a true friend—and then has to protect him from a hunter.

Sasquatch: The Legend of Bigfoot

This one's about seven men who venture into the wilds of northwest Canada. It's another one that looks like a documentary, though it's not. There are, however, simulated bear attacks (done using a trained grizzly and a Tootsie Roll).

The Sasquatch Gang

A group of friends find sasquatch footprints in the woods, and while a team investigates, some neighborhood dummies try to make money from the sasquatch. This one's rated PG-13 for some crude humor, so keep that in mind.

Not Your Typical Bigfoot Movie

For an actual documentary, you might try *Not Your Typical Bigfoot Movie*, an award-winning production about two real bigfooters in an economically depressed Ohio town. It's a story about bigfoot on one level, but also about big dreams and the meaning of friendship.

SPOTTED!
Too Fast to Hunt

In the northeast corner of Utah, near where the borders of Wyoming and Idaho intersect, are mountain ranges thick with deer and elk, which the *Finding Bigfoot* team believes to be a staple of the Sasquatch diet.

It's also a favorite spot for hunters such as Bryce Chestnut, who was in the region for the second time, walking along a hillside, when he heard branches breaking and crashing sounds coming from a nearby ravine.

He put his binoculars to his face, looked down, and saw something black race by.

"I could see it was on two legs," he said. "It came running through this brush and crashed into this clearing, went over the top and was gone into the trees."

By the time he'd grabbed his rifle, the creature was gone. But he has no doubt what he saw. "The only thing it can be in my mind is bigfoot."

BIGFOOT JOKES

How do you keep a bigfoot from smelling?
Plug her nose!

Why did the sasquatch cross the road?
So he could eat the chicken.

Knock, knock.
Who's there?
Squatch.
Squatch who?
Gesundheit!

Bigfoot and the Easter Bunny had a race. Who won?
Bigfoot, silly. The Easter Bunny doesn't exist!

Why did the world's fastest runner refuse to race bigfoot?
Because he was afraid of defeet.

What did bigfoot do to the mosquito?
She squatched it.

What car does bigfoot want to drive?
A toe truck.

Why did the bigfoot talk back?
Because she was a sass Squatch.

What sport is bigfoot best at?
Tracks-in-field.

How did the yeti know what time it was?
She checked her sasq-watch.

MORE BOOKS TO READ

Bigfoot
by Stephen Krensky
Lerner Publications, 2007
This is a compact book about bigfoot that covers lots of interesting facts. It's a straightforward introduction to the topic.

Bigfoot Exposed: An Anthropologist Examines America's Enduring Legend
by David J. Daegling
Altamira Press, 2005
Daegling does not believe bigfoot exists. He uses his background as an anthropologist to examine evidence for the creature—especially tracks and the gait displayed in the Patterson-Gimlin film— to form counterarguments to the claims made by Grover Krantz, Jeffrey Meldrum, and other colleagues who find the evidence of bigfoot to be compelling. This is a good book to read to understand how the same evidence can be read in different ways.

Bigfoot: The Life and Times of a Legend
by Joshua Blu Buhs
University of Chicago Press, 2009
This book has a lot of great information about bigfoot, the history of the creature, and the attempts that have been made to find one. Another skeptic, Buhs argues that bigfoot is a legend with particular appeal to society's least powerful men.

Giants, Cannibals & Monsters: Bigfoot in Native Culture
by Kathy Moskowitz Strain
If you're interested in learning a lot about Native American tales about bigfoot, this book is a great choice. If there truly were no North American apes, you will wonder what on earth might have inspired these stories.

In Search of Sasquatch
by Kelly Milner Halls
This book is full of great information from people seriously pursuing sasquatches: cryptozoologists, linguists, anthropologists, biologists, and more. There's a particularly interesting section on bigfoot in folklore. The author has written other books about cryptids, so if you're interested in more about undiscovered animals, you might check out her work.

Sasquatch: Legend Meets Science
by Jeffrey Meldrum
Jeffrey Meldrum is one of the nation's leading bigfoot researchers. He's a professor at Idaho State University, an expert in bipedalism and foot morphology, and a tireless seeker of the facts about bigfoot. This book is full of detailed and compelling arguments about the creature, and it also rebuts some arguments made by people who think bigfoot is nothing more than legend.

Bigfoot: The Yeti and Sasquatch in Myth and Reality
by John Russell Napier
Dutton, 1973
This book is one you'll probably have to find in a library, as it's decades old. But it's important for the historical record. John Napier was one of the world's leading primate researchers. He wrote about the Patterson-Gimlin film, which he believed was probably a hoax, but concluded that there was no way to prove that conclusively.

Sasquatch: The Apes Among Us

by John Green
Hancock House Pub, 2006
John Green is a journalist who's spent his whole life collecting stories of bigfoot encounters. He worked closely with every significant bigfoot seeker of the last several decades, and he's written several books about bigfoot. This one is considered the definitive account. It's hard to come by, but you might find a copy at your library.

The Scientist Looks at the Sasquatch

(Volumes I and II)
by Grover Krantz and Roderick Sprague
University Press of Idaho, 1977 and 1979
These books are collections of articles by anthropologists about bigfoot. Because they are by scientists for scientists, they are not light reading and have lots of nitty-gritty detail. But if you want to know how anthropologists go about their work, you might go to a library and check one or both of these out.

HELPFUL WEB SITES

You can go online to learn more about bigfoot, examine footprint casts and pictures, watch videos believed to be of the creature, report sightings, and stay current with the latest news. Here are some good places to start:

Animal Planet | Finding Bigfoot

animal.discovery.com/tv-shows/finding-bigfoot
Find plenty of information about the show, exclusive videos, data on sightings and tracks, as well as a place where you can share your own evidence.

Bigfoot Lunch Club

bigfootlunchclub.com
When there's bigfoot news or research, the Bigfoot Lunch Club is likely to have it.

Bigfoot Field Researchers Organization

BFRO.net
This is Matt Moneymaker's group, and their Web site has information on thousands of sightings, plus insight about bigfoot gained from analyzing the many sightings that have occurred. It's a great place to start your research and report sightings.

Bigfoot Information Project

bigfootproject.org

Go here for interviews with top researchers and investigators.

Bigfoot Sounds

bigfootsounds.com
Listen to excerpts of the Sierra Sounds, a famous exchange of what is believed to be multiple bigfoots talking.

North American Bigfoot

northamericanbigfoot.com
This is Cliff Barackman's blog. He has field notes from the *Finding Bigfoot* show. It also links to his main site, CliffBarackman.com, where you can report encounters, look at his huge collection of casts, read articles, and watch instructional videos.

Bigfoot Books

bigfootbooksblog.blogspot.com
This is the blog of a Willow Creek, California, bookstore that specializes in sasquatch literature.

Bigfoot Encounters
bigfootencounters.com
You'll find news, sightings, articles, and scholarly musings about all aspects of bigfoot.

Bigfoot Times
mcclean.org/bigfoottimes/index.html
A variety of information about bigfoot, from news to new books to events. It's managed by longtime bigfoot scholar Daniel Perez.

Crypto Zoo News
cryptozoonews.com
Longtime bigfoot and general cryptid expert Loren Coleman gives regular updates about bigfoots and other undiscovered animals.

Facebook Finding Bigfoot
facebook.com/FindBigfoot
This Facebook group posts pictures and videos and offers analysis of them.

THE SMITHSONIAN ON THE YETI

What does the foremost Museum of Natural History in the United States have to say about the yeti? A lot, as it turns out. Here's a form letter the museum sent in 1988 in response to the many inquiries people had about the creatures:

The Museum of Natural History often receives requests for information concerning the "abominable snowman," "yeti," "sasquatch," or "bigfoot," and other unknown creatures said to exist in certain mountain regions of the world, particularly the Himalayas, western Canada, and northwestern United States. Though the term "abominable snowman" can refer to all these creatures, generally the terms "snowman" and "yeti" refer to an Asiatic creature, while "sasquatch" and "bigfoot" refer to North American creatures.

The actual existence of a "snowman" has not been definitely proven. Most evidence submitted so far is based on photographs of previously unknown animal tracks, unusual scats (dung), and some hair samples. Among the many explanations offered on the basis of the above evidence, one that has appealed greatly to the popular imagination, is that the animal in question is a huge, human-like ape, or possibly a surviving race of early man. Because of its terrifying aspect, the animal,

supposedly of Himalayan origin, came to be called "abominable snowman"; it is this intriguing name that is probably responsible for such widespread interest in these creatures in various parts of the world.

Many zoologists who have reviewed the evidence have come to the conclusion that the tracks of the Himalayan "snowmen" were really made

by bears, monkeys, or other already known animals. A few disagree, saying there is little similarity. The tracks attributed to the sasquatch of the northwestern United States are much more human-like but of vast proportions (fifteen to eighteen inches in length). With the large publicity the "snowman" has received in recent years, many popular articles of little scientific value have been written. Some of these are convincing to read, but they are mostly based on circumstantial evidence of "sightings," tracks, hair, scats, and some doubtful pelts and skull caps.

While most scientists believe the likelihood of the existence of such a creature is small, they keep an open mind, as scientists should. One cannot prove anything on the basis of negative evidence, and the only satisfactory proof that an animal fitting the description of the "snowman" exists would be either to capture one and study it or to find undisputed skeletal evidence. Only these kinds of finds would result in the universal recognition of the "snowman" by all scientists.

Below is a list of references through which you can pursue this topic further:

Byrne, Peter. *The Search for Bigfoot: Monster, Myth or Man?* Washington, D.C.: Acropolis Books Ltd., 1975. (Summary of the evidence collected over the years by a believer in the "snowman's" existence.)

Halpin, Marjorie and Michael M. Ames, eds. *Manlike Monsters on Trial: Early Records and Modern Evidence.* Vancouver: University of British Columbia Press, 1980. (Explores Sasquatch-like creatures and summarizes reports of sightings.)

Hillary, Edmund and Desmond Doig. *High in the Thin Cold Air.* New York: Doubleday and Co., 1963. (The famous Mount Everest climber recounts searches for the "snowman" in the Himalayas.)

Izzard, Ralph. *The Abominable Snowman Adventure.* Toronto: Modder and Stoughton, 1954. (Concerns the search for the "snowman" in the Himalayas.)

Napier, John. *Bigfoot: The Yeti and Sasquatch in Myth and Reality.* New York: E. P. Dutton, 1973. (An eminent primatologist discusses his views on the possibility of the "snowman's" existence. Concludes no hard evidence exists though allows for some soft evidence.)

Sanderson, Ivan T. *Abominable Snowmen: Legend Come to Life; The Story of Sub-Humans on Five Continents from the Early Ice Age Until Today.* Philadelphia and New York: Chilton Co., 1961. (Sifts the accumulated evidence for and against the "snowman's" existence rather thoroughly. For a critical comment on this book, see Carleton S. Coon's review in the January 1962 issue of *Natural History* magazine.)

Sprague, Roderick and Grover S. Krantz, eds. *The Scientist Looks at the Sasquatch.* (*Anthropological Monographs of the University of Idaho*, no. 3.) Moscow: The University of Idaho Press, 1977. Collection of articles first published in *Northwest Anthropological Research Notes.*)

Suttles, Wayne. "On the Cultural Track of the Sasquatch," *Northwest Anthropological Research Notes.* 6(1):65 90, 1972. (Discusses Native American views of the Sasquatch. Article also in Sprague.)

PUBLIC INFORMATION OFFICE
DEPARTMENT OF ANTHROPOLOGY
SMITHSONIAN INSTITUTE

PHOTO CREDITS

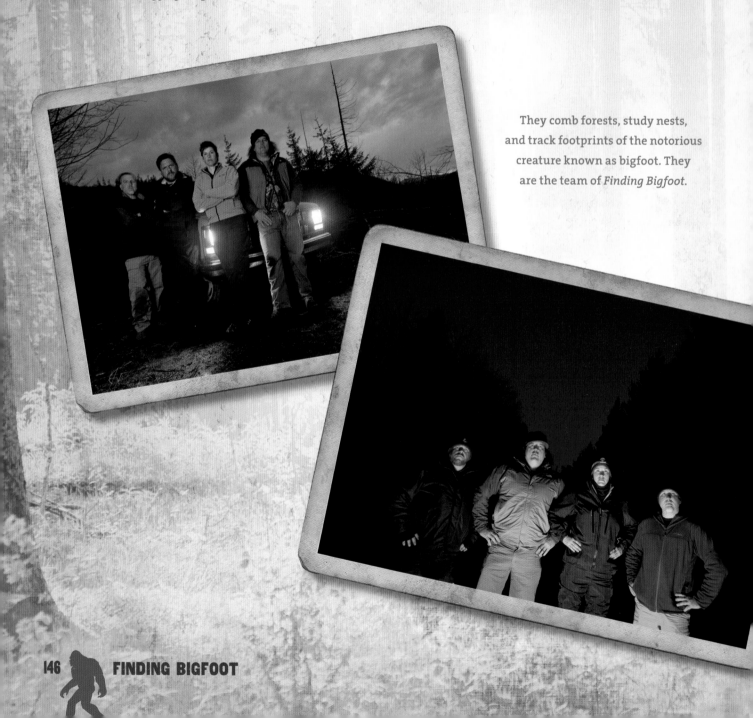

They comb forests, study nests, and track footprints of the notorious creature known as bigfoot. They are the team of *Finding Bigfoot*.

ACKNOWLEDGMENTS

About ten years ago, I almost didn't receive an email that would change my life.

Troublesome Internet monkeys had rerouted the message to my junk mail folder, and I was just about to click the delete button when I noticed an interesting subject line: literary agent?

As it turns out, the email was from Erin Niumata, who'd read my educational humor column on Encarta, loved it, and thought I had a book in me. Over the years, Erin has given me endless encouragement, support, and great advice. She was also correct in her diagnosis. It was a book in there. Or two! And perhaps many more, which beats intestinal parasites every time.

Thanks, also, to my other literary agent, Jill Corcoran, for being a mom and a sister and a friend . . . and also very fierce about the details.

I'm grateful to the team at Feiwel and Friends for knowing I was the right writer for this book, and for doing such a beautiful job with the design and packaging. Special thanks to Anna Roberto and Jean Feiwel for their terrific support.

To the kids in Ms. Monroe's class at Hamlin Robinson School in Seattle, your questions made a huge difference. Thank you, Tyler, Sam, Kellen, Lee, Sophie, Emily, Isabella, Lucy, Vanessa, David, Luke, Matthew, and Kyle.

To my writing friends, most especially Sean Beaudoin, Kevin Emerson, and Cat Patrick. You turn this solitary slog into a hilarious adventure. More, please.

To Adam, Lucy, and Alice for your love, patience, and willingness to listen to all of my bigfoot jokes. I promise I'll stop . . . eventually. To Graham and Rosie, you are good dogs.

And finally, thank you to everyone seeking sasquatches, both literal and metaphorical. To chase after something while others doubt takes courage. Whatever your dream is, keep after it.

—Martha Brockenbrough

INDEX

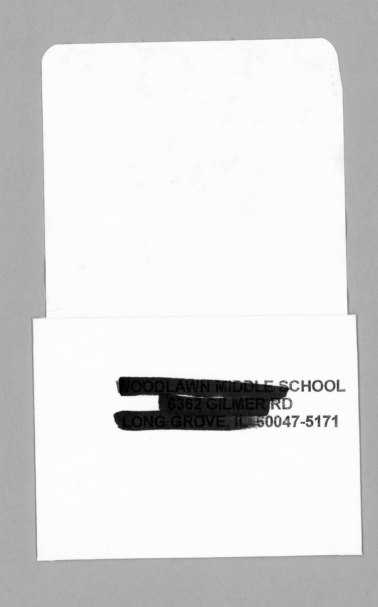

WOODLAWN MIDDLE SCHOOL
6362 GILMER RD
LONG GROVE, IL 60047-5171